JIM HARMON'S
NOSTALGIA
CATALOGUE

JIM HARMON'S NOSTALGIA CATALOGUE

Published by J. P. Tarcher, Inc., Los Angeles
Distributed by Hawthorn Books, Inc., New York

To Kris and Lil Neville,
without whose good will, encouragement,
and basement storeroom this book
would not be possible.

ACKNOWLEDGMENTS

Special thanks to Forrest J. Ackerman ("Mr. Science Fiction"), Richard Gulla (authority on stage magic), Paul Kalin (author and actor), Donald F. Glut (foremost authority on the Frankenstein legend), Ron Haydock (rock music performer and novelist), Kirk Alyn ("Superman" of the serials), Bob Greenberg (animator and film director), and Malcolm Willets (Disney authority and bookseller), whose contributions to this book may not be entirely visible but are greatly appreciated.

My appreciation is also extended to Dave Amaral, Jack Bennett, Frank Bresee, Skip Craig, Gerry Kramer, and all the other collectors and dealers cited elsewhere in these pages who helped me assemble my collection of nostalgia.

For the book itself, thanks to Rick Greenberg for his photographs (with some additions by Lloyd Nesbitt), to Frank Lane for the cover and overall design, to Nancy Bryan for copy editing, and as usual, to Jeremy Tarcher for his creative contributions.

J.H.

Designed by Frank Lane

Published by J. P. Tarcher, Inc.
9110 Sunset Boulevard,
Los Angeles, California 90069

Library of Congress Catalog Card No. 73-83281
ISBN 0-87477-013-0

Manufactured in the U.S.A.

Published simultaneously in Canada
by Prentice-Hall of Canada, Ltd.,
1870 Birchmount Road, Scarborough, Ontario

10 9 8 7 6 5 4 3 2 1

TABLE OF CONTENTS

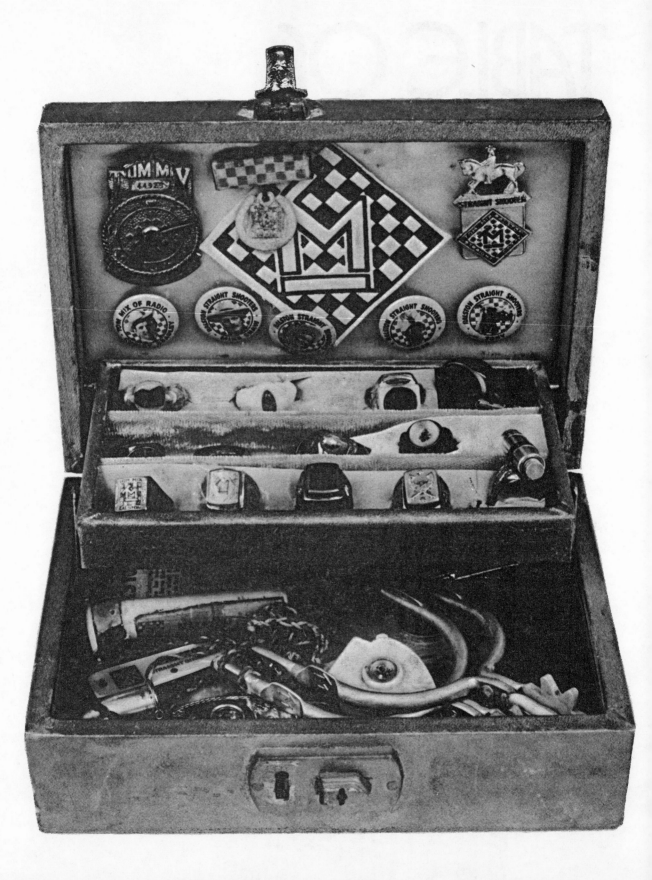

INTRODUCTION

HERE'S AN OFFER YOU WON'T WANT TO MISS! YES, WE WILL MAKE YOU A KID AGAIN!

Simply tear the top off your mundane, workaday world, do not mail it—throw it away—and return with us to Checkerboard Square, St. Louis, Missouri; Battle Creek, Michigan; Chicago 77, Illinois . . . addresses whence came all the badges, the rings, and the fabulous premiums of Tom Mix, Buck Rogers, Captain Midnight, and other great heroes of radio.

Just as the ghost of Christmas Past took Ebenezer Scrooge to all his old haunts, we will take you to the wonderful addresses of your childhood:

Detroit, Michigan—home of the Johnson Smith Company, purveyors of the Ventrilo, joke rats, live baby alligators, and complete plans for building a two-passenger airplane (25¢).

Plymouth, Michigan—location of the Daisy Manufacturing Company, makers of Red Ryder cowboy carbines and Buck Rogers No. U-235 Atomic Pistols.

Hollywood, California—the source of even more magic than the state of Michigan, the provider of Saturday afternoon movie serials and cowboy pictures, Buster "Flash Gordon" Crabbe, Johnny "Tarzan" Weissmuller, and, a bit later, such Saturday morning television epics as *Space Patrol* and *Sky King.*

Those marvelous places don't exist any longer, at least not as they once did, but we can take you back because we *saved* all the stuff they produced!

Collectors save things. They speak of *saving* old comic books, *saving* match books from the 1939 New York World's Fair and the Stork Club, *saving* movie star photographs. They save *things* because they can't protect the past they loved from the rush of the present or from the looming engulfment of the future. Collectors are not necessarily political conservatives—they are *conservationists,* conserving the best of the past for themselves and others.

Who would want to save the bread lines of the thirties, or the newspaper headlines about Pearl Harbor? We want to preserve memories of Jimmy Cagney and Edward G. Robinson as champion gangsters, Little Orphan Annie Shake-Up Mugs, the Lone Ranger's stirring "Hi-Yo Silver!"

Nostalgia is composed of things of the past we like to remember; history is composed of things we would like to forget.

Nostalgia is infectious. It can even be caught by persons too young to have actually been there themselves. In a typical letter I received after the publication of my book *The Great Radio Heroes,* a 17-year-old boy wrote: "It must have been worth going through World War Two to be able to listen to *The Lone Ranger* and *I Love a Mystery* on the radio; I wish I could have."

Many unpleasant things happened in the thirties and the forties. There are unhappy things about growing up in any era. You are too fat or too skinny; you have to wear glasses or braces on your teeth; you simply cannot learn to spell; and that special person you adore thinks you're a creep. Life is always tough, but the fun things of the thirties and forties make it endurable. You throw away the geography test with a grade of 63, but you keep the Tom Mix Whistling Siren Ring. You remember the radio story of how Tom used the ring to summon the Straight Shooters to his rescue. You remember sending in your dime and a box top from Ralston, and waiting for the ring to come. You remember getting it, opening the brown envelope, and wearing the ring for a few days until you went on to something else. Even so, you knew the ring was worth saving.

Most of us saved lots of other things as well—everything from Dixie Cup lids (with pictures of movie stars on them) to stamps. In fact, I can recall a boyhood experience with stamp collecting, which says something about the young collector's compelling urge to write off for anything and everything, just to get a piece of mail of his own.

I had seen an ad in the back of a comic book. It looked innocent enough. It said something like:

> TEN FAMOUS NUDES. THREE AMERICAN PRESIDENTS. THE CHAMPION RACE HORSE OF ALL TIME. HUEY LONG. SENATOR ALBEN W. BARKLEY. HENRY FORD. EINSTEIN. SALLY RAND. GET THEM ALL *on approval!*

It was not an advertisement for some wild party —one with some awkward pairings in the corner. No, it was offering an enticing set of stamps. Of course, you got them only on approval, but if you were nine or ten years old, you were pretty sure you would approve of them. A couple of weeks after sending for them, you got three or four sheets of paper with stamps attached. The stamps had prices under them: 85¢ for a Ruffled Hungarian, $4.90 for a Peruvian Suede, $11.20 for a Scalloped Highlander. The instruction sheet said to send back any stamps that you did not want, but they all looked pretty keen—especially the nude Mona Lisa from France; the Brazilian half-cent with a portrait of our President Hoover, sabre in hand, astride his great black stallion; and the Panama blue showing a peasant removing his straw hat and kneeling to kiss the hand of President Hoover (this one was labeled "Inter-Hemisphere Friendship").

After you had had your terrific stamps a couple of weeks, you received another letter from the stamp dealer. It went like this, more or less:

> Dear Sir: You have had time to fully evaluate the fine value we have made available to you. We will appreciate your full and immediate payment for all stamps not returned to us in the specified approval period. Failure to comply will result in grave consequences to your whole credit structure and will be a mark against you the remainder of your life. Please send us a check for $213.45 by return mail.
>
> Very truly yours,
> A. M. Gordon, President
> APEX STAMP & RUBBER NOVELTY CO.

$213.45!

Your dad probably did not even *have* that much money. Who did? Who could have?

Your forehead and your palms were sweating. There was simply no way for you to send them the money. They didn't want the stamps back—you had gone over the "approval" period. Besides, you weren't quite sure where all those stamps were, although you knew the dog had chewed up some of them. There was nothing to do but wait . . . wait for the police, perhaps even the FBI, to pull up in front of your house or pluck you off the school playground and take you to jail.

In another week, there came another copy of the same letter from the Apex Stamp & Rubber Novelty Co., except that this copy was printed on bright, flaming red paper. Even the envelope was red. Across the letter, in what looked like handwriting in purple ink, was scrawled: "This is your second chance! Warning—you will not get another!"

Two letters! But after all, you thought, what could they do? They were way off in Elizabeth, New Jersey. You were safe. Let them send a lot of letters. It didn't matter. Still, the worm of fear gnawed at you.

Then it came.

It was a large, square envelope, very stiff, very heavy. The paper had a rippled texture like leather. You opened the envelope by breaking two daubs of something like wax into which had been imprinted a lavish "A." You removed the folded paper inside, paper of the same textured weave. It made a large, impressive crackling sound as you flattened out the sheet. The writing was apparently by hand, with the broad strokes of a quill pen. At the bottom of the letter was a seal the size of a silver dollar, bearing the same impressive "A" monogram as the seals on the envelope. This seal supported a length of crimson velvet ribbon that hung down past the bottom of the unfolded letter. It read:

To the Transgressor: Greetings:

Ye who have transgressed against the Apex Stamp & Rubber Novelty Co. be given

NOTICE

that your deeds are known to Those who Must Know of these things; that there has been kept a record and that this record will be kept; that you are known and shall be known. Be it known that if you fail to send in payment of
$213.45
or some part of it, then shall befall penalties upon you. Heed and comply before it shall be past all redeeming.

Signed and Sealed with My Talisman,
The Official Adjudicator of the Right

Blood drained from your head, leaving it as empty as a schoolhouse in July.

This was it. There could be no doubt. You had received a letter from God.

With death and indubitable damnation facing you, the situation called for the most desperate of all childhood moves: you would have to tell your folks about your trouble.

Your father heard the story and read the letter. He gathered up all the stamps he could find, shoved them in an envelope, and briskly wrote out a note to Mr. A. M. Gordon telling him that if he ever sent any more threatening letters to his son, he would go personally to Elizabeth, New Jersey, and punch Mr. Gordon through the nearest wall, pointed head first.

Still, there did come another letter from the Apex Stamp & Rubber Novelty Co. Avoiding parental advice again (of course), you opened it and read:

Dear Customer:

Thank you for accepting our generous settlement agreement and sending us $5.00. Rest assured this will not be a mark on your record.

Hoping to serve you again, I am

Most sincerely,

A. M. Gordon, President

APEX STAMP & RUBBER

NOVELTY CO.

This letter certainly was not as ornate as the one from the Official Adjudicator of the Right. It was just a printed form, black on white paper, of which they must have had a lot made up. They had even sent the wrong one, for your father had *not* sent $5.00.

As the years went by, I received a few other letters urgently insisting on payment. They were for boxes of salve I had *not* been able to sell to my friends and neighbors and thus Win Big Prizes (my friends and neighbors seemed not particularly in need of salve), and even, in later years, for books and records I had not received or even ordered. None of them, however, was quite as impressive as that letter from the Apex Stamp & Rubber Novelty Company. Now *there* would be a collector's item! It would be impossible to give it a price, but it should be worth at least $213.45!

Who *could* give a price to any of these recollections or to any of the things of childhood (except perhaps dealers in them)? They are beyond price.

I'm not sure what price a dealer would place on my old display box of premiums. It would probably please a pre-Reformation Midas himself. The box itself I picked up for a dollar in an old junk store only two years ago. Some of the rings and badges and miscellany it now contains have been mine since I was a kid; others have been bought or traded for in the last few years.

The original articles had moved from my dresser drawer back in Illinois to a portable metal filing case in my Hollywood apartment, and finally to the old jewelry case. I was aware of the incongruity of placing what some would consider junk in a case for jewels, but my main pleasure was that it offered a *display* of the contents.

With a flip of a latch I could display dozens of memories and dreams, a parade of years from President Roosevelt to President Eisenhower, from Hal Kemp to Elvis Presley. That box is part of my life. It may be worth looking into from time to time.

I hope that this book will prove such a box of premiums for you.

RADIO PREMIUMS

Before Blue Chip stamps, red and white checkerboard Ralston box tops brought free gifts.

These box-top gifts were more important than a new alarm clock or coffee table. Life itself often depended on box-top gifts. How many times did Tom Mix have to summon Tony the Wonder Horse with his Whistling Siren Ring to carry him to safety from a den of rustlers or the leaping flames of a forest fire? When Jack Armstrong, Uncle Jim, Billy, and Betty walked the deathtrap-strewn path that led to the treasure of the Lost Temple of the Mugwumps, did they not do so with the aid of Jack's trusty pedometer? This miraculous instrument allowed them to measure the distance between the Pit of Vipers and the Well of No Bottom with precise accuracy, thus escaping an untimely end. Could these fabulous items do less for us?

If, after school, you happened to spot a Nazi spy in front of the Sugar Bowl Cafe, it was a darn handy thing to have a Captain Midnight Signal Mirror to flash a sunlight message into the eyes of the nearest F.B.I. agent. These were things that no amount of money could buy.

Of course, you had to send that Wheaties box top, or Ovaltine label, or Ralston pouring-spout seal, maybe even a dime. But what really brought you these priceless treasures was your *loyalty* – loyalty to Tom or Jack or the Captain or the Lone Ranger, and to the cereals that carried their seal of approval. It was loyalty to what each of these heroes stood for—plenty of fresh air, soap, and exercise; fair play; and the belief that Straight Shooters always win.

The price of loyalty is high for a grown-up, but for the small boy or girl who lies dreaming inside, the price is so low as to seem itself a gift. As you turn these pages, don't regret not saving those prizes. Today they would be only small bits of metal and plastic, but, where it really counts—in memory and imagination—these gifts, which no amount of money could buy, are forever yours.

One source was more bountiful than all others in supplying these gifts to us, often completely free of cost, and I think it natural to go back first to that series.

TOM MIX

STRAIGHT SHOOTER GEAR

The *Tom Mix* radio program offered the greatest variety of premium rings, badges, and toys of any source from the thirties into the fifties. Tom seemed so compulsive about offering to his Straight Shooters that he was still at it *two years* after the radio show went off the air in 1950. In the early fifties Ralston cereal boxes and comic book ads had "The Tom Mix Trading Post" offering some of the last radio gimmicks, plus some new ones, such as the Tom Mix Glowing Belt and the Tom Mix T-shirt (actually sporting a photographic likeness of the radio actor who played Mix, Curley Bradley). Apparently the factory designing the stuff had been working far ahead, and hadn't counted on Ralston dropping *Tom Mix* after nearly twenty years for a new radio and television show, *Space Patrol.* That was the end of the trail—the hoofbeats of Tony the Wonder Horse were drowned out by the roar of rocket engines.

The trail started back in 1933. The first Mix radio premium is thought to have been the Horseshoe Nail Ring. It was a horseshoe nail you were supposed to bend into a ring by use of pliers and a poker, an item for a more rural, industrious time. You received instructions in the first manual along with the ring. This, like most Straight Shooter manuals, was devoted to telling you how great the real-life Tom Mix was—soldier of fortune with Teddy Roosevelt's Rough Riders in Cuba, in the Boxer Rebellion in China, during the second Boer War in South Africa, then cowboy, sheriff, U.S. Marshal, Texas Ranger, rodeo champion, and movie star. Tom Mix was made into a legendary figure.

Unfortunately, it was almost all legend, not fact. Some kids believed the legend (a few, like the present writer, until they were almost forty), but legend it was. A recent book by Tom's distant cousin, Paul E. Mix, called *The Life and Legend of Tom Mix,* documents the famous cowboy star's life with official government records and proves he served only one hitch in the U.S. Army, during the Spanish-American War, and never left the

country for any foreign entanglements whatsoever.
Furthermore, he served as a town marshal only in
Dewey, Oklahoma, for a short period around 1910
(mainly dealing with bootleg whiskey in a dry
state) and, later, as a construction camp "marshal"
and prohibition agent. As for the legend, it was
all—almost all—dreamed up by publicity agents
over fifty years ago. It was a dream of godhead
carried on the shoulders of one lonely human
being. Personally, I prefer to recall the story in my
Ralston Straight Shooters Manual, with its "Tom
Mix Chart of Wounds" showing twelve bullet
wounds and forty-seven bone fractures (not
shown were twenty-two knife wounds or the
four-inch hole in his back caused by a dynamite
explosion). The story in the manual may not have
been the truth, but it was better than the truth—
it was adventure, excitement, impossible idealism.
Now that I know the true story, I shall certainly
do my best to forget it.

THE COMPASS-MAGNIFYING GLASS

The Tom Mix radio series lasted for so many years, with its tales of the Old Wrangler, the kids Jimmy and Jane, the cowpoke Pecos, and the black cook Wash, that the sponsor repeated several premium offers at long intervals. The Compass-Magnifying Glass exceeded this repeat schedule. The first one offered by Tom Mix in 1937 was of silver-like nickel, with a tiny compass set in a metal oval, and a magnifying glass that could be folded back inside the oval. This bore no identification, such as the famous Tom Mix TM-Bar brand. It was probably available in department stores as well as for a box top and ten cents from Ralston. (Today, several dealers are offering a similar but *not* identical compass-magnifying glass, purporting to be the 1937 original, and selling it for thirty-five dollars. The *imitation* is made of metal as thin as a sheet of paper and has the words "COMET-JAPAN" in a boxlike design. The *original* 1937 model is of metal as thick as heavy pasteboard and has the single word "JAPAN," not in a box, on the back.)

Only two years later, the radio show offered a brass Compass-Magnifying Glass that was much handsomer. It still had a compass set in metal, with a magnifier that folded back inside, but now the gold-colored brass was decorated with western designs: a rope border on the front encircling a six-gun, a steer skull, and a horse's head. On the back was not only the TM-Bar brand, but the words "RALSTON STRAIGHT SHOOTER."

It was nearly ten years before the Tom Mix show thought the market might need another Compass-Magnifying Glass. The plastic age had arrived by then, and the most popular plastic used in radio premiums by *every* show was the kind that stored up energy in the light and glowed in the dark. The plastic Compass-Magnifying Glass was formed in the shape of an arrowhead, a popular design for several Tom Mix items. It bore the TM-Bar brand in a rope-like script.

For nearly twenty years the Mix show had given away compasses and other radio series made similar offers. Did Tom Mix think his Straight Shooters were always getting lost and needed his help in getting home? Quite probably some of those who lived in small towns or on farms had got lost out in the countryside on Boy Scout outings or lone ventures. Fewer listeners in the big city had this experience, I suppose. Yet the compass expressed the outdoor atmosphere of the show, the clinging to tradition of the frontier, and was a symbol of showing us "the right way to go," as Tom Mix's Straight Shooters credo was supposed to do in other aspects of life.

THE COMPASS-GUN

The most unusual compass offered by the Ralston show (or probably by any other) was the Compass-Gun, a 1½-inch replica of a six-shooter. It was made of plastic (which glowed, of course) except for the metal barrel, which was a magnet that pointed north when allowed to swing from the chain attached to it. The other end of the chain was fastened to a tiny glow-plastic arrowhead that was also a whistle. The chain could be fashioned in one way to make a key-chain for boys, in another to form a bracelet for girls. One of the last offers of the radio series, it was the first Tom Mix premium in some fourteen years not to bear the TM-Bar brand or some other Mix identification. Perhaps someone had seen the writing on the wall and left the Mix brand off so that the premium could be offered later by some other radio or television show.

THE SIGNAL ARROWHEAD

The Signal Arrowhead was large—4½ inches long—and made of clear plastic that, incredibly, did *not* glow in the dark. This gadget had a magnifying lens, a reduction lens (termed a "smallifying" glass), a set of musical pipes or whistles, and a spinning whistle siren like those used on several other Mix premiums (the Dobie Sheriff's badge and the Siren Ring, for example).

THE WOODEN SIX-SHOOTER

"I'll give you this gun!" Tom Mix told his loyal Straight Shooters in 1936. "I'll send you this exact wooden model of my favorite six-shooter. It's brand new, never been offered before . . . steel-black with ivory-colored wood handle. Cylinder turns like a real revolver. A real cowboy gun for only one Ralston box top and 10¢ in coin to cover packing and mailing costs. Hurry!"

Radio fans need not have hurried too fast. The wooden six-gun, with various modifications, was offered until 1942. It wasn't really brand-new in 1936 either, having been offered as far back as 1933. Yet even in an era of relatively inexpensive metal cap-guns, this wooden model attracted kids. It somehow looked more like a real gun than the flashy chrome jobs of the singing cowboys; what's more, it broke open and the cylinder spun. It was lightweight, easy to carry, and *almost* free. Above

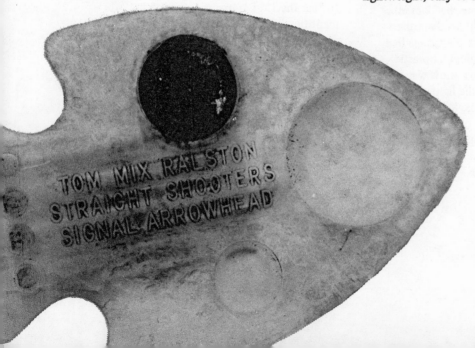

all, it was touched with the magic of Tom Mix. With the *real* six-shooter that served as a model for this wooden copy, Tom could perform such feats as "the mirror shot." ("Tom Mix, sighting through a mirror, fires his six-shooter over his left shoulder and snuffs out a candle held by a girl standing twenty feet behind him. . . .") Wow! Tom certainly had to be a good shot and to have a gun like this swell six-shooter. After all, he had "been blown up once, shot twelve times, and injured forty-seven times in movie stunting," not to mention his twenty-two knife wounds. With luck, and this wooden gun, you could lead a life just like Tom's.

Several different models were issued over the years. The earliest was as large as a real gun and looked authentic, with a barrel that broke and a cartridge drum that spun. In 1933, this was the only toy gun many kids had. It was free, costing not even a dime for handling and mailing—only a box top. By 1939, the Tom Mix gun had shrunk to a size not much bigger than a derringer and was just one solid piece of wood. Furthermore, it cost a dime.

The idea of the gun was dropped after this. More elaborate and fancier shooting irons were available in stores for perhaps two or three dimes, and more people had dimes to hand out to their kids as the forties drew near. (Any of these guns today is worth about four hundred dimes—forty dollars.)

THE TELEGRAPH SIGNAL SET

"Tom's Postal Telegraph Set is a dandy—comes complete with international code," all Straight Shooters were told in 1938. "Any pal who eats Ralston can get my Signal Set *free,*" Tom Mix added.

This model was only a mechanical clicker in a cardboard box, but it was a lot of fun in those pre-World War Two days. On the radio show, messages would be clicked out which you could decipher if you had the "secret" Morse code printed on the Signal Set. (In the show itself, Tom Mix's personal set was a deluxe model, *not* precisely like the one sent out through the mail. Tom carried his set around in his hip pocket, and it was a *wireless* model that could pick messages out of the air.)

The offer proved to be so popular, like many others on the Mix show, that a telegraph set was again offered in 1940. This one was an "electric" model, complete with batteries. "Get your neighbor to send for one, too. Then you can hook both sets together and send and receive messages between your house and the house next door. .." They really worked, too. And the set was "free for two Ralston box tops, or one Ralston box top and 10¢ in coin." Because both models were essentially cardboard "paper" items, not basically metal or wood, they were very fragile, and are among the rarest items to collect today. Their current collector's value is anything from fifty dollars upward.

THE IDENTIFICATION BRACELET

"Both boys and girls will like this nifty silver-flashed identification bracelet. The checkerboard design band will remind you of the red-and-white box of scrumptious Hot Ralston every time you look at it. Yessirree! It has your very own initial on it and your own number listed in Tom Mix's identification bureau. So if you ever get lost and can't remember your name, just go to the nearest policeman and ask him to find out from the Tom Mix Ralston Straight Shooters. BONUS: With your bracelet, you will also receive a genuine fingerprint file card. Put your own fingerprints, name, and address on it and this card will be sent right to J. Edgar Hoover's F.B.I. offices in our nation's capital. It's official! Isn't that swell?" It cost one Ralston box top and 15¢.

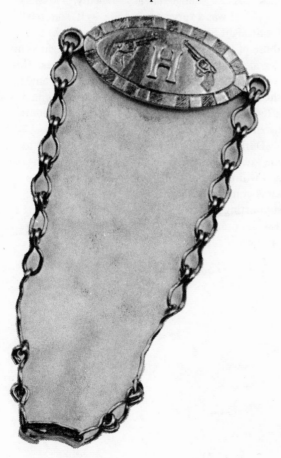

MORE BRANDED MERCHANDISE

The TM-Bar brand appeared on a number of badges over the years. One of the earliest was the Straight Shooters Campaign Medal (inspired by military campaign decorations) showing a figure of Tom on Tony above a checkerboard field with TM-Bar cluster. It was a nice-looking badge, although it did not decode, whistle, hum, or explode. It proved popular enough that it was offered in both a gold and a silver color model. (Variations on it also included a Ranch Boss badge, and a Wrangler badge.)

In 1940, Ralston offered the first and only Tom Mix Decoder Badge. The dial indicator was a movable six-shooter that pointed to symbols like a horseshoe, a skull, or a star, which stood for messages like "danger ahead," "enemy," "keep going." It was a very simple code, as if Tom felt his Straight Shooters were even younger than those of Orphan Annie and Captain Midnight, who decoded complicated number-letter messages. This was a totally unfounded assumption. The Tom Mix show was always the best written and performed afternoon serial, and had more teenage and adult listeners than any other.

During World War Two, the series returned to the idea of a military decoration with a ribbon (red and white checkerboard), allegedly made by the same company that made Army service ribbons, supporting a horseshoe-shaped "medal" sporting a TM-Bar brand, and made of the familiar glowing plastic.

Finally, in the last few years of the show, there came a set of five Ralston Straight Shooters buttons, showing photographic likenesses of Sheriff Mike Shaw, Wash, Jane, Tony the Wonder Horse, and—not exactly Tom Mix, but the radio series star, Curley Bradley, the Tom Mix of Radio. On the back of each button was a single code word, such as "danger ahead," etc. The signals had not changed much in this game in ten years.

The likeness of Curley Bradley was replacing that of the movie star Tom Mix in some Ralston ads. There was probably some intention of putting the personable former movie stunt man into a Tom Mix television series, but, if so, it never materialized.

The face of the real Tom Mix was used by Ralston all through the thirties and into the forties. In 1935, the sponsor offered a Tom Mix Western Movie Reel. You turned a handle and rolled past a viewing window a series of still pictures showing highlights of such Mix films as *Rustlers' Round-up* or the serial *The Miracle Rider.*

After the radio show went off the air in 1950, Ralston continued its connection with its famous radio show by boasting a picture of Tom Mix—the real Tom Mix made famous again through TV showings of his old movies—on the front of the cereal box for years.

THE RINGS

Rings were the most frequent premium offered by the *Tom Mix* show and by most other radio serials as well. Besides being a piece of jewelry, a ring is most often a mark of identification. For grown-ups a ring may identify their marriage status, their college, their lodge, or some other organization.

On one level, kids wanted to imitate their elders with their own "lodge" rings, but, on a second level, they wanted to identify themselves with the radio characters they loved. Despite the knowledge that they weren't grown-up organizations, kids wanted to show themselves as part of Tom Mix's Straight Shooters or Captain Midnight's Secret Squadron. A pin-on badge could offer equal identification (and they were popular), but somehow a ring had more class.

The first Tom Mix offer of all in 1933, the Horseshoe Nail you bent yourself into a ring shape, was followed by many others.

Shortly after the first Horseshoe Nail Ring, the Ralston series invited listeners to send for a TM-Bar Checkerboard Emblem Ring. It was the basic Tom Mix ring, showing only his famous brand against Ralston's checkerboard trademark. Like most premium rings, the gold-colored ring "adjusted to fit any finger" by having a band of two overlapping strips of metal that could be pulled apart or pushed together to assure a fit—or a pinched finger.

In 1935, you could obtain a Tom Mix ring that bore not Tom's initial but your own on top (with the TM-Bar brand on the sides). It was presented as a good luck charm that *might* bring you some of the same luck that had saved Tom Mix in numerous dangerous confrontations with outlaws and grizzly bears. (Statistics are not available on how many kids, confident in the possession of their own Tom Mix Initial Good Luck Ring, tried to fight bears with no weapons save their rings.)

The only interesting new item of the early forties was a Tom Mix Signature Ring with a reproduction of Tom's autograph in a silver-like metal crest.

After being off the air a season or so, the radio series was revived in 1945. Curley Bradley, who had played the guitar-strumming sidekick Pecos, moved up to the title role, replacing deeper-voiced Russell Thorson. There were other changes in the show's format, too. The Old Wrangler disappeared and was replaced by another old-timer, Sheriff Mike Shaw, but there were still premiums aplenty, including more rings.

After the Siren Ring came the Tom Mix Magnet Ring, sporting a block magnet on top, which was especially helpful in picking up paper-clipped secret plans on the sly. It may sound unlikely, but in a newspaper ad Tom rescued the plans for the atomic bomb in this way!

The Look-around Ring had a tiny mirror inside that let you peek around doorways before exposing yourself to the bullets of any rustlers hiding near the schoolhouse.

Another Whistle Ring followed—this time a slide-whistle, which was actually too large to be worn as a ring. (It was nothing, however, compared to the gigantic Sky King Teleblinker Ring.)

The final Tom Mix ring was the Tiger Eye Ring that glowed in the dark. It was a handsome ring, combining transparent plastic with a luminous base and actually looking like a cat's eye. But the band was made of another cheap, golden plastic. It looked like something that might be found inside a cereal box, as compared with the earlier sturdy metal rings that really looked as if they were worth a dime and a box top.

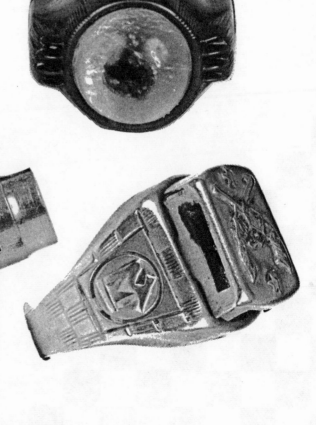

OTHER STRAIGHT SHOOTER GEAR

One of the glow-plastic offers was a set of Tom Mix Spurs, made of solid metal with the TM-Bar brand stamped into the sides, but with pointed rowels of glowing plastic. They were one of the larger and more elaborate premiums offered in the last years of radio drama, harking back to such premium toys of the thirties as the Tom Mix Telegraph Sets (two varying models) and the Tom Mix Blow-Gun Set.

Over the years, the premiums generally got smaller and cheaper, yet one of the last Mix premiums was the Bullet Telescope, over four inches long, with a bird-call device that slipped inside when not in use. Apparently you were supposed to call the birds, wait until they came, and then get a good look at them with the telescope. (Lucky Tom Mix used the telescope on the radio show mostly for spotting gunmen lying in wait for him in the rocks overhead.)

Among the last few premiums was a toy television set that was a viewer for films showing photographs of the radio cast (not in the least disillusioning—the radio cast could have done a television version easily), Tom Mix mysteries in comic-strip form, or other pictures. With a radio show admitting that its listeners' interest was in TV sets (the radio show even made reference to old Tom Mix movies playing on television) radio drama series did not have long to last, and the *Tom Mix* show came to an end in 1950.

During the eighteen-year period the show was on the air, *Tom Mix and His Ralston Straight Shooters* offered scores of premiums. They were all great. The degree of greatness depended on just what age you were vhen they were offered, and your interests at the time. Most of these premiums are sold for around thirty dollars apiece today, but they were worth a million dollars to us back then.

22

THE MYSTERY RING

Of all those rings and badges and toys that we eagerly dispatched our box tops for, the Tom Mix Mystery Ring seems to be the most difficult to dig out of the past, the dusty attic of once-useful junk. You have to go through many of those attics to find the door to 1939. There inside—don't step on that roller skate, don't knock over the life-size cardboard figure of Johnny calling for Phillip Morris or a stack of *The Saturday Evening Post* or an El Supremo cigar box—in a dented Prince Albert can, *there* you may find the magic ring of the man who (on screen and radio anyway) would never have helped empty any of those tobacco containers, Tom Mix.

The ring bears his brand on top, the fabled TM-Bar. The simulated gold band that fits any finger holds a little box with a little hole. Inside the little hole, you see a photograph of Tom Mix and his Wonder Horse Tony, magnified "100 times." The photo is signed To my Straight Shooter Pal, Tom Mix.

I remember the day I received my ring in the mail. I was about six years old. Eagerly, I tore open the small brown box, and unwrapped the ring from a list of the old premiums you could still send for (and which I already had), and looked into the hole to see Tom Mix blown up one hundred times. There was nothing inside! Could Tom Mix have gypped me? I looked harder. There *was* a little speck. That little speck did sort of resemble a man riding a horse, I thought. Was the ring broken, I wondered? Or were they all like this?

Disheartened, I took the problem to my dad. He explained to me carefully that advertising often makes things sound a lot better than they really are. I could not expect the ring to be really as great as they said on the radio. My father examined the ring for himself. He looked in and said, "Why,

there he is, James!" I looked inside. Sure enough, there was Tom Mix standing next to Tony, seemingly as big as life. Tom Mix had not cheated me. Maybe you could not believe everything everybody said on the radio, but you could trust Tom Mix. My problem was that I had looked into the wrong hole, the one in back that was just to let in the light. When looked at from the right angle, it was all as clear as day.

I wore the ring or carried it in my pocket for months. Then one day I forgot to take it out before my mother put my pants in the washer. The laundering washed out the picture of Tom and Tony completely. Sadly, I threw the ring away, because it didn't "work" any more. No doubt I could still have sent for another one. I could have hounded my mother for another box of Ralston, but maybe I was a little tired of the ring after all, a little bored with it.

About twenty years ago, I started to look for another copy of that Mystery Ring. Recently, a young man in Wisconsin, who had seen my ad in a collectors' magazine, wrote that he had found one in the family attic. I sent him the price agreed upon and, in a far shorter time than you had had to wait for Ralston to get around to sending your package, a medium-sized brown box arrived. Eagerly I tore it open and removed the ring from the layers of cotton and tissue paper in the old cuff-links case it had been packed in. There was the TM-Bar brand on top. I put the ring up to my eye. *I couldn't see a thing!* Had the ring been broken in transit? There was nothing inside, except a little speck.

"Why, there he is, James!"

I reversed the ring and looked into the right opening. Yep, there were Tom and Tony. The passing of thirty-odd years had touched them lightly, but the world had changed a lot for me. I had learned many things, one being not to leave *this* Tom Mix Mystery Ring in the pockets of any pants I shipped home for my mother to launder for me.

Beyond its place in my personal history, this particular ring is one of the most difficult of all box-top giveaway items to locate today, possibly because part of it is made of glass, or a glass-like plastic. That part must have had a hard time withstanding the use children made of it and their universal temptation to throw the ring away once the magic picture was broken. In any case, you can frequently find Little Orphan Annie rings nearly ten years older than this Mix premium selling for ten dollars or so, whereas the Tom Mix Mystery Ring is difficult to find and, when found, may be priced at well above a hundred dollars. I paid eighty-five dollars for mine. The second one, that is. For the first one I paid a dime.

The Tom Mix Mystery Ring is only a token of childhood, but it is so rare and sought after that it might be known as the Mixese Token. Thirty years ago, only the photograph of Tom and Tony was blown up a hundred times. Today, collectors and dealers have blown up the *price* nearly a thousand times.

26

THE LONE RANGER

The mark of the true intellectual is being able to listen to the *William Tell Overture* without once thinking of The Lone Ranger. I never can, and I would think anybody who does is so culturally alienated that it must be difficult for him to function in mid-twentieth-century American society. To me the music was never cheapened by its association with the Lone Ranger. He is as mythic a figure as Rossini's Swiss patriot—perhaps even grander. William Tell may have shot an apple off his son's head, but the Masked Rider fired countless bullets in the cause of justice, never once taking a human life. In fact, splitting an apple with an arrow pales beside just one of the feats of the tall masked man on the white horse who rode through the night to warn peaceful settlers and Indians at a harvest celebration of an attack by "a bunch of half-breeds and white renegades," urging his great stallion, "Faster, Big Fellow, faster. The lives of Tonto and the people in the valley depend on us. Come on, Silver! *Hi-Yo Silver, Away!*"

Today, "image" is everything in public life. Actors and politicians pay out tens of thousands of dollars to people to create images for them. Some, of course, had an image without any effort at all: Humphrey Bogart, Marilyn Monroe, Jimmy Cagney. But nobody in the nonvisual medium of radio has had such a powerful image as the Lone Ranger. And that image was given him by the staff of radio station WXYZ in Detroit.

In the winter of 1932, the station owner, George W. Trendle, had the idea of creating a new Western series and got together with two others to do it—a young writer named Fran Striker, whom he had brought in from Buffalo, and the WXYZ station manager, named Brace Beemer. According to Beemer, Trendle contributed the basic concept of the series and Striker followed his lead. Beemer himself contributed several details—and later his voice—to the character.

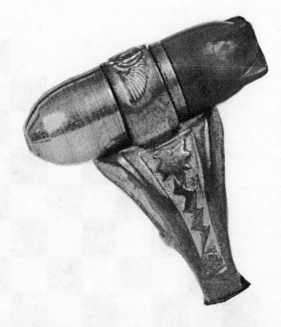

The idea for the masked man was based on Zorro, the masked avenger of Old California, created by novelist Johnston McCulley and played in silent films by Douglas Fairbanks Sr. In an earlier account, I wrote that Fran Striker wanted to make the Lone Ranger a laughing trouble-shooter like Zorro and that Trendle wanted to make him a grim, avenging angel of justice. I then suggested ironically that there was a "compromise" in which the Lone Ranger lost his sense of humor. The late Mr. Trendle, then nearing ninety, wrote me that there was *no* compromise. According to him, "What I said went!"

Anyway, Trendle and his staff together worked out all the details that have become so familiar to us, and the show went on the air in early 1933. In the first seven episodes, the Lone Ranger was played by a man vaguely referred to by Trendle and Beemer as "Deeds" or "Jack Deeds." In recent years, a gentleman named Lee Trent has shown up on radio and TV interviews claiming to be that first "Mr. Deeds." There do not seem to be any exact records on this point. In any case, the first actor in the role was soon replaced by George Stennius (now George Seaton, the movie director). When he left several months later, Brace Beemer took over the part of the Masked Man for the better part of the first year, although he soon left the show to set up his own advertising agency.

This rapid turnover in the cast was owed primarily to the wages Trendle paid. While radio performers' salaries were not very high anywhere in the industry, they were held to an all-time low by Trendle. An actor working for him got perhaps five dollars a week for doing three broadcasts— about $1.65 a show. The writers fared somewhat better, but they had to make six or eight carbon copies of their manuscripts so that Trendle would not have to pay to have them mimeographed for the cast. (The actor who got the last carbon had to be damned good at ad libbing.) Later, the activities of the unions made things better, but even then the star of the vastly successful *Lone Ranger* show got only $150 a week when even minor comedians were pulling down $5,000 a week.

When I pointed out some of these things in my book *The Great Radio Heroes,* George W. Trendle objected. He also seized on a few errors of fact, such as my giving the impression that Fran Striker was the sole writer of *The Lone Ranger* and that Trendle had him chained up somewhere grinding out three scripts a week ("an impossible task," according to Trendle). However, I remembered that George Lowther was able to turn out three half-hour scripts a week for the *Tom Mix* radio series during the 1949-50 season, most of which were of a high caliber for the genre. When I corrected the mistakes in the paperback edition, Trendle expressed his gratitude by offering to do me a favor—any favor I could think of.

I decided to start big. I told him I had always wanted to have a print of *The Green Hornet* movie serial (worth perhaps five hundred dollars). I asked for the *Hornet* since Trendle still controlled the rights to that series, though he had sold everything on *The Lone Ranger* ("every scrap of paper") to the Jack Wrather Corporation. Trendle told me he would be happy to give me a print of the *Hornet* film—even his own personal file copy—but, alas, he had none. Anything else he could do for me? I said I would like to have one of the Green Hornet rings that had been given away on the radio show. Trendle replied that he would love to send me this small token but that they had given away all of them long ago to "the boys and girls of America." He added that he understood such mementoes had become "quite valuable" in recent years (in other words, I wasn't going to take him). In the end, he gave me his "heartiest thanks."

Nevertheless, I am grateful to have had a correspondence with a man whose projections of his ideals so profoundly influenced American culture, and my own life as well. And it is a pleasure to lay to rest the allegation that George W. Trendle was a tight-fisted old son of a gun.

Brace Beemer returned to the role of the Lone Ranger in 1941 upon the accidental death of Earle Graser, who had taken the part for some years. It was Beemer who continued in the lead until the series ended its live broadcasts in 1954 and went into reruns on radio, where it continues to this day. (The series was actually off the air only about five years, from 1957 to 1962.) Beemer appeared in many parades and rodeos riding a fine white horse he called Silver's Pride (another way of saying Silver's son), which most people took to be Silver himself. The white stallion outlived Beemer, who died in 1965.

The Lone Ranger had so many regional sponsors offering so many versions of the same safety badge, mask, and toy gun that it would have been impossible to keep track of all of them. Bread companies seemed to adhere to the Masked Rider of the Plains with doughy persistence. His first regional sponsor was Silvercup Bread (no, the bakery's name was merely a fortuitous coincidence). Silvercup cautiously offered a painting of the Lone Ranger, and the deluge of letters received convinced them of the character's appeal. Silvercup then started a safety club with various badges, club cards and manuals. Another bread company, Marita, which sponsored the show in the Southern states, offered a black cardboard Lone Ranger mask. (But who wanted to wear a mask reading "Marita" right between the eyes?)

When General Mills took over coast-to-coast sponsorship of the Lone Ranger in the forties, they solicited box tops from Kix, Cheerios and Wheaties for the rings and other goods they offered. During World War Two, the Lone Ranger offered a patriotic ring emblazoned with a variety of emblems of each of the armed services. (When you slid the top back, you found a tiny photograph of the Masked Man, too.) A later ring was a tiny filmstrip viewer with scenes of the Marines landing on Iwo Jima. That may seem rather far removed from the Wild West—but another Lone Ranger ring sported a tiny model of the atomic bomb (though the front part of the bomb looked more like a shiny silver bullet). When the red plastic tail fins of the bomb were removed, you were supposed to be able to see light flashes from disintegrating atoms inside. For some reason, this ring seems to be the most common of all radio premium rings; I have seldom seen a dealer's or collector's display without one.

The front part of the atom-bomb ring was certainly not the only silver bullet offered by the Lone Ranger. One of the earliest was hollow and contained a lump of genuine silver ore inside. A later, blunter model followed in a few years, also hollow and containing two tablets to be dissolved in water—one to make invisible ink, the other to make what you wrote visible. The top part of the bullet also contained a tiny compass as an extra dividend. The silver bullet motif was carried over into toys sold in stores—a cartridge belt full of silver bullets to go with a gun and holster set, and another set with a belt "loaded" with silver bullet pen and pencil. Yet another radio premium was a ring topped with a model of the Lone Ranger's six-shooter. The gun even shot sparks when you fanned its flint wheel.

But the most sought-after of the Masked Man's premiums is a model of Frontier Town, where the Lone Ranger and Tonto occasionally settled down for a few months, apparently as a relief from traveling the entire length and breadth of the West. The models of the buildings appeared on the backs of a series of Cheerios boxes. To complete the model, you had to send in for certain parts, like the gigantic map (about three by four feet) on which the model buildings stood. Then you could follow the Lone Ranger as he left Sheriff "Two-Gun" Tyler's office, rode out past the general store and the livery stable, took a short-cut through the Union Pacific tunnel and met Tonto in front of Rustler's Cave. I had the whole town, put together on an unused kitchen table on our screened-in back porch. But then the Lone Ranger moved out of Frontier Town, and I changed from twelve to thirteen. Not without regret, I gathered up Frontier Town one day and dropped it into the wastebasket. Today I regard my action as a bit ill-advised, since I could probably get a couple of hundred dollars for the models. Still, although Frontier Town was a nice place to visit, I wouldn't want to live there.

JACK ARMSTRONG,
THE ALL-AMERICAN BOY

The year 1933 was a great one for classic radio serials. It marked the beginning of *Tom Mix, The Lone Ranger*, and *Jack Armstrong, the All-American Boy*. The name Jack Armstrong has entered the language, replacing the dime novel hero Frank Merriwell as the symbol of the idealized young American male. There has never been a real move to replace Jack with a newer image of virtue. I suppose the only near comparison might be singer Pat Boone, and he is a man with grown-up daughters. So Jack Armstrong would seem assured of retaining his position for some time to come.

Everything said about Jack Armstrong was true, and of course everything said was to the good. There has never been a purer-hearted hero. The Lone Ranger was a symbol of virtue, but somehow (on radio, at least) he rose above being a mere symbol and took on the characteristics of a real man. Jack was never gifted with a personality—just purity. His sidekick, Billy Fairfield, did have some human failings. But where he was frightened, Jack was calm; where Billy was overly curious, Jack was patient; where Billy was impetuous, Jack was restrained. No wonder the Fairfield family allowed Billy's sister, Betty, to travel into the farthest jungles with Jack. No tropic moon would make his blood pressure rise or libido tremble.

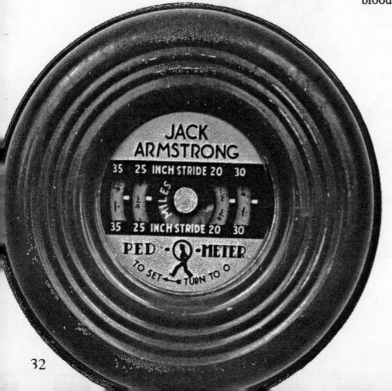

Of course, when we were children, Jack's perfection did not seem impossible. Some day, when we got around to it, we were going to be that perfect, too. Certainly it was what our parents expected us to become.

Jack never seemed as energetic in giving away premiums as did Tom Mix. Perhaps giving away things seemed too un-American to him: kids should work for what they got. But then a high school student had less money to spend on gifts for his friends than did ranch owner. While Tom Mix was giving away full-size wooden replicas of his six-gun, Jack Armstrong was offering photographs of the cast.

As the thirties wore on, however, Jack got more into the spirit of things, and toward the end of the decade he offered what was probably his most popular premium.

THE PEDOMETER

"Here's your chance to own this amazing instrument, scientifically designed, sturdy construction . . . Just hang pedometer on belt or pocket . . . and hike. It'll keep track of every step you take! Lots of fun to watch! Counts every step! Have your gang guess how far it is to camping grounds. Prove with pedometer who's nearest right!"

This gadget, divorced from the exciting violence of guns and knives, proved popular with two generations of Jack Armstrong radio fans, and even later with other youngsters. You could buy a "professional" pedometer for a few dollars at the store where you got your Boy Scout supplies, but Jack Armstrong offered you *his* model for a Wheaties box top and 10¢ in 1939.

Jack's own pedometer played an intricate part in the radio serial, of course. Using it, Jack was able to follow the instructions in an old pirate map and keep Billy, Betty, Uncle Jim and himself on the correct course out of the bottomless-pit death traps laid by the Cult of the Crocodile God. Listeners were immediately convinced of the pedometer's usefulness.

The pilot model of the device was labeled "Jack Armstrong Pedometer." Later versions became Wheaties Pedometers—and, still later, Lone Ranger Pedometers and Sergeant Preston Pedometers—when the device was offered by other programs sponsored by General Mills, makers of Wheaties. The latest (but probably not the last) version of the pedometer, still with essentially the same design, was available on certain cereal box backs in 1970 as the "Wheaties Hike-o-meter" for a box top and one dollar. The value of Jack Armstrong's original model today is somewhere between twenty-five and fifty dollars.

HUDSON HIGH CLASS RINGS AND OTHER THINGS

The All-American Boy also offered one of radio's most appropriate premiums—a sound effects kit. Among the things the package contained was red cellophane to crinkle up to make a sound like fire (the red coloring was probably essential). Another item was a balloon which, when you blew it up and let a pebble roll around inside, simulated the rumble of thunder. Not included was a fifty-watt solid state amplifier which would have helped those effects a lot. But when you were a kid, your own imagination supplied a good deal.

Jack was a pioneer in offering glow-plastic premiums, a standard of the art. About 1935 he offered a luminous plastic copy of the fabled "Iron Key" that played a significant part in one of his radio adventures in far-off India.

In another story, a wise lama gave Jack a "Magic Answer Box" which would suggest an answer to any question put to it. It was like a Ouija board. A dial on the little red box had an arrow pointing to such replies as "Yes," "No," and "Perhaps." The heat of your thumb caused a cellophane strip to push the arrow over in varying degrees, producing varying answers. Its main use was in revealing how wise lamas solved the riddles of the universe.

A trip to mysterious Egypt opened the way for an offer of an Egyptian ring with a siren whistle on top, another trail-blazing device. Countless later premiums also sported the spinning whistle on rings, badges and tops of pencils.

A journey to the Sulu Sea involved a luminous ring with carvings of crocodiles on the band holding a stone in their jaws. Naturally it too was a premium offer. The Wheaties folks must have ordered enough rings for every finger in America. An existing series of recordings of the show during this period reveals an increasingly frantic quality in their pitch for the ring. Finally, the announcer, silken-voiced Franklyn McCormack, was urging listeners to send in for *two* rings, one to wear on either hand, so that you could give the appearance of *two* glowing cat's eyes in the dark.

During World War Two Jack Armstrong's premiums took on a military aura. There was a series of cardboard airplane models you punched out and assembled. In later years, such things would come right in (or on) cereal boxes, but at that time you had to send in a box top for each model, or at least for each pair of them. "Have you got your Jap Zero and Grumman Hellcat yet?" we were asked. (That was one of the few times "Hell—" was ever heard on the *Jack Armstrong* show, or on any other old radio program.)

Another premium involving wartime aviation was the Jack Armstrong Secret Norden Bombsight. It was a wooden box that let you look down at toy ships below through a mirror arrangement and then drop little red bombs on the cardboard cut-outs. *Wham!* There goes a Nazi U-boat! *Blam!* There goes a Jap troop carrier—score a thousand kills. Kids had a lot of fun back then.

The rationing of metal for the home front cut down all premium offers during the war, but shortly afterwards the Armstrong series advertised an Explorer's Sun Watch. It was a sundial, resembling a pocket watch, with a compass added to the face. But it was not a Jack Armstrong premium *per se*—it was a Frank Buck Explorer's Sun Watch and bore his name.

At this time, Frank Buck did not even have his own radio show, but his old jungle documentaries like *Bring 'Em Back Alive* were being re-released to movie theaters. Old Bring-'Em-Back-Alive himself appeared once on the *Jack Armstrong* program in a capsule interview, a rather disillusioning one. The announcer asked him what his most hazardous experience had been. "I've never been in any real danger in my life," Buck snapped. "Only fools who take stupid chances and don't make sound plans ever get into danger." To the best of my recollection he was never invited back.

Was Jack Armstrong's name losing luster when they had to bring on a big name to sell a premium on Jack's own show? Apparently it was. Before too many more seasons had passed, Jack stopped traveling the seas and jungles with Uncle Jim, Billy and Betty, and settled down in the U.S., taking a job with the Scientific Bureau of Investigation. Soon the once-famous name of "Jack Armstrong, the All-American Boy" was dropped from the program's title and the series officially became *Armstrong of the S.B.I.* Armstrong, the federal agent, never offered one premium, not so much as a telephone-bugging kit for junior operatives.

S.B.I. Agent Armstrong was forgettable. It is Jack Armstrong, the All-American Boy, we remember, with his Pedometer for measuring every jungle trail and his hopes for a bigger, finer America that would be a friend to the whole world.

CAPTAIN MIDNIGHT

SS-1—or, as he was known to less than intimates, Captain Midnight—issued a lot of equipment to his faithful Secret Squadron members. He was quite a bit behind all the gifts that Tom Mix made to his Straight Shooter pals, but then Captain Midnight was on the radio for significantly fewer years.

The very first Captain Midnight premiums were offered not by Ovaltine, his long-time sponsor, but by his original patron, the Skelly gasoline company —even before the organization of the Secret Squadron, when the Captain's group was known only as the Flight Patrol.

THE FLIGHT PATROL MEDAL

Early Flight Patrol premiums included a winged badge with a litmus-paper insert that turned a different color when the humidity got high enough to indicate rain. There was also a 1940 Flight Patrol Medal, about the size of a half-dollar but gold-colored. One side had a clock design with the hands at midnight, the other a three-bladed propeller; between the blades there were tiny *bas relief* heads of a helmeted Captain Midnight and his two kid assistants, Chuck Ramsey and Patsy Donovan (a forerunner of Joyce Ryan, who did not sound so relentlessly Irish). The original of this medal usually goes for ten to twenty dollars.

An exact replica of the Flight Patrol Medal is now being offered—with a tiny, scrupulous "R" (for replica) added—with the cooperation of both the Skelly and Ovaltine companies by Mr. Peter Collinson, 2040 S. Summerton Rd., Mt. Pleasant, Michigan, 48858. Along with the medal—solid metal—comes a handsome two-color certificate of membership in the Flight Patrol and a brief history of the *Captain Midnight* radio series. This set,

which costs only three dollars, is highly recommended to all interested parties.

A far less successful replica set is being offered as a bonus with several Longines Symphonette records (chiefly of the big bands of the forties). It consists of a reproduction of the 1942 Captain Midnight Code-o-graph badge in raised cardboard (but it is only a *picture* of the real thing, not an exact copy) plus a Secret Squadron Flight Commander certificate (actually from the *television* series) and a paper-thin recording, 45-rpm size, of the first episode of *Captain Midnight* on the network for Ovaltine (but not the *very* first episode of all, done for Skelly gasoline). These cheaply made items can also be purchased for $3.50 from a source other than Longines: write Old Abandoned Warehouse, P.O. Box 595, Old Chelsea Station, New York, N.Y. 10011. (Longines does not sell the set, but only offers it periodically as a "free" bonus with the purchase of at least $11.92 worth of records.)

Captain Midnight items are natural choices for re-issue as replicas, for—in the sense of having the largest circulation—they were probably the most popular of all. The chief reason for this was that Secret Squadron equipment was generally absolutely *free*. Kids needed only a three-cent stamp and a label from a can of Ovaltine to send for Captain Midnight's stuff.

In the early years, Ralston had offered a number of Tom Mix premiums free of cash, only requesting a box top, but by the forties most radio shows asked for proof of purchase and the familiar "ten cents to cover the cost of handling and mailing."

Only Ovaltine refrained from asking for coins. (Of course, a can of Ovaltine cost a lot more than a box of cereal: in 1941 Wheaties cost about a dime a box, and a large container of Ovaltine was sixty cents. Getting the Ovaltine was hard enough for some kids without the extra dime.)

THE CODE-O-GRAPHS

The most popular Captain Midnight premiums came along in 1940, when Ovaltine assumed sponsorship of the radio series for the new fall season. Best of all were the Code-o-graph badges. Codes were popular not only with *Captain Midnight* listeners but with the fans of other shows and the readers of pulp magazines like *The Shadow*. The talisman—badge or ring—and the secret code all suggested a secret society. It was a natural. All children live in a secret society, protecting their privacy and their dreams from the enemy—the grown-ups. Such items as Captain Midnight Code-o-graphs were only instruments to express an already existing order of furtive signals and knowing glances.

The first Code-o-graph boasts an eagle and looks a bit like a police shield except for the center dial with its circle of numbers and letters. It was issued late in 1940 for the year 1941 (dated ahead just as car models are).

The 1942 Code-o-graph was a particularly good one, with a photograph of Captain Midnight inserted above the code dial. (The square-jawed photograph must be of some male model, since it is not of Ed Prentiss, who played the role on radio, or even Dave O'Brien of the movie serial.) Because of metal rationing during World War Two, there were no Code-o-graphs issued in 1943 and 1944.

Unlike the green Lucky Strike package that went to war and never returned, Code-o-graphs snapped back in 1945 with a model offering a magnifying glass in the center of the code dial. No doubt this came in handy for reading coded messages that were printed very small, or spelled out in pinholes, as was recommended. The 1946 Mirromatic Code-o-graph is, in my opinion, the most handsome of all. From a winged star, the caption "Captain Midnight's Secret Squadron" sweeps majestically around the code dial. In the center of the dial, on the knob, is a small mirror: ideal for flashing code messages. (This was actually the last pin-on badge offered.)

The next Code-o-graph was a police whistle with the code dial on one side and the winged clock insignia on the other. It looked different, but that was about all that could be said for it. The 1948 version was metallic, but completely round. It always reminded me of a girl's compact (not a favorable impression to a young boy). On the back was another mirror, larger than the one of the 1946 badge but not as nice-looking. The last radio Code-o-graph came in 1949. It was called the Key-o-matic and it was a nice item. An oblong device to be carried in your pocket, it was actually a code machine requiring a small key to operate. The Key-o-matic was a winner. A fitting closing for the Captain Midnight era on radio. (Later, the TV series of *Captain Midnight* offered some small Code-o-graph badges made out of gold or silver plastic. They were fairly handsome, but much cheaper than the sturdy metal Code-o-graphs offered on radio.)

The Code-o-graphs, when available from dealers, go from twenty-five dollars up. But even rarer and more valuable than the Code-o-graphs themselves are the instruction manuals that went with them. These handsome booklets were originally digest-size, then in 1947 were cut to half that size. They were lithographed in full color on good paper and had full-color paintings (not just line drawings) of Captain Midnight, Chuck and Joyce, and their enemies, Ivan Shark, his daughter Fury, and their henchman Fang.

The "1942 Book of Official Charts, Codes and Secrets" is an especially handsome book full of such character paintings, plus the secrets of the Secret Squadron—made even more secret by being printed in mirror image so that no outsider casually looking through the book could figure them out. The back cover is terrific—a poster of Captain Midnight, Uncle Sam, and a Father and Mother (surely the greatest four living Americans) gazing down benevolently on Girl and Boy Scouts drinking Ovaltine.

Captain Midnight made other premium offers than the Code-o-graphs and manuals, of course. There were Flight Commander badges that you could get only after you had joined the Squadron and recruited three other new members. There were rings: a Queen of Sheba Ring, an Aztec Ring, and others. There were several Shake-Up Mugs and drinking cups, like Little Orphan Annie's. These are all valuable and sought after, but it is the Code-o-graphs that are the truest symbols of Captain Midnight and his Secret Squadron.

Captain Midnight's
SECRET SQUADRON
1942 BOOK OF OFFICIAL
CHARTS, CODES AND SECRETS

THE CAPTAIN MIDNIGHT SHAKE-UP MUG

"Have you heard the news? The news about that marvelous new two-piece, bright-colored Shake-Up Mug that Captain Midnight has for you?" radio announcer Tom Moore inquired enthusiastically. "That big, handsome two-in-one shaker-upper you use to make ice-cold chocolatey shake-ups to drink every day? Well sir, Captain Midnight has one for you almost as a gift. You can't buy one in the stores at any price. They're *patented* and made only for Captain Midnight and his Ovaltine-drinking pals. Why, if we sold one to an outsider, our regular price for this big, handsome, two-piece Shake-Up Mug would be fifty cents—but *you* can have one for fifteen cents and the label from your jar of Ovaltine . . . "

Captain Midnight's Shake-Up Mug was a blue-capped reddish plastic cup used to shake up powdered Ovaltine with milk and crushed ice to make a cold health-food drink. The Ovaltine Shake-Up Mug was the most durable premium of tne radio era; in fact, it lasted all through it. Actually, Ovaltine was offering Uncle Wiggly drinking mugs for their product even before commercial broadcasting. Little Orphan Annie offered her mug in 1930, and repeated the offer up until 1940 when Captain Midnight took over. The Captain's drinking container was the last of his radio premiums (1950), offered at the same time as it was being offered on the short-lived *Captain Midnight* television program. Ovaltine offered another Shake-Up-Mug in connection with the Olympic Games in the mid-sixties.

For pure commercial exploitation, the Shake-Up Mug was undoubtedly the most ingenious premium ever offered on radio: you spent your money on the sponsor's product to send for an item that helped you to use more of the sponsor's product.

Shaking up a mug full of Ovaltine was something that kids really liked to do, maybe because it seemed like having a milk shake at that emporium of delights, the corner soda fountain. (In fact, the commercial assured you that the mixed Ovaltine was "just like a creamy milk shake.") In a small way, having an Ovaltine Shake-Up Mug was like having a soda fountain right in your own home.

For faithful fans in the thirties and forties, the Shake-Up Mug offered a "host of healthfulness" (as Annie attested) and many "happy landings" for members of Captain Midnight's Secret Squadron. Grown-up collectors are willing to pay ten to thirty-five dollars to recapture the creamy delights of that era.

LITTLE ORPHAN ANNIE

Little Orphan Annie, "the chatterbox with pretty auburn locks" who had a dog named Sandy that said "Arf!" and could tear your arm off, was the leading character in the first afternoon radio adventure serial. (Although *Let's Pretend* did start earlier with half-hour versions of fairy tales, and although there may have been some kind of show on a local station, *Annie* is the first one that really counts, the first that had staying quality and influence.) Naturally she offered the very first premium. Nobody seems to have entirely accurate records, but this premium seems to have been the Little Orphan Annie Shake-Up Mug. If it wasn't the first, it should have been.

The Wander Company, makers of Ovaltine, took Little Orphan Annie out of Harold Grey's *Chicago Tribune* comic strip and put her on the air in 1930, first in Chicago, with Shirley Bell in the title role. Another later version originating from San Francisco featured Floy Margaret Hughes as Annie.

Most of Annie's early adventures took place in Simmons Corners, with her friends Mr. and Mrs. Silo and the boy Joe Corntassel. All in all, the show did not have a strong appeal for big-city apartment dwellers, since it consisted largely of "adventures" such as Annie and Joe's getting lost in the woods, or the haystack catching on fire.

Such stories were enough to drive anyone to drink, and Ovaltine came to the rescue with their Shake-Up Mug. The idea was not entirely new to them. In the twenties, before radio became very important, Ovaltine had offered a Shake-Up Mug identified with Uncle Wiggly, the kindly old rabbit of children's books. But now radio became the perfect medium to sell a mug for Ovaltine.

Announcer Pierre Andre told us of one of several models of the mug in his soft but intense voice: "It's Little Orphan Annie's very own Shake-Up-Mug. . . With a beautiful, new and different picture of Annie and Sandy right on it. . . You put the special orange shake top on when you shake up your ice-cold Ovaltine, then lift the top off, and presto! You have a special Little Orphan Annie mug to drink right out of . . .

Here's the way you get it... Take out all of the thin aluminum seal you find under the lid of a can of Ovaltine and mail it, together with ten cents—one dime—to cover the cost of mailing and handling—to the Wander Company, 180 North Michigan Avenue, Chicago, Illinois. Then in a few days the postman will bring you this brand new Little Orphan Annie Shake-Up Mug to have and keep for your very own."

Soon the Wander Company apparently found that the listeners needed something more than a free mug to keep their attention from wandering. Daddy Warbucks entered the scene (played by Stanley Andrews, later the Old Ranger on TV's *Death Valley Days*) and took Annie and her friend Joe on adventures around the world on his yacht.

Daddy Warbucks' character was somewhat mellowed on radio from what it was in the comic strip. According to the latter, he had made a vast fortune from munitions (war bucks, get it?) and had used this wealth to create a private army to murder anybody who got in his way. His chief henchman, the giant Punjab, used his scimitar to slice off the heads of his master's enemies. The cartoon would show their heads neatly separated from their bodies by several inches, their hair standing on end in fright and still miraculously with breath enough to scream "YIIII!" The scene was always good for a laugh.

Of course, Warbucks had a heart of gold—he could afford to buy the best—and he used a fraction of a thousandth of one per cent of his fortune to support an orphan girl—every once in a while, that is. (Apparently most of the time he sent her packing to walk the roads of America alone, except for old Sandy.)

The typical way to get Warbucks out of the story line for a while was to have him ostensibly murdered by one of his many enemies. Months later, of course, we learned that "Daddy" had miraculously escaped from the exploding airplane or the burning house or the sinking ship. (Annie always refered to "Daddy" with those quotation marks around his name. No wonder *Mad* magazine chose the most vulgar interpretation of their relationship.)

COLD OVALTINE SHAKE-UP MUG

LEAPIN' LIZARDS! FOR A REAL TREAT YUH CAN'T BEAT A COLD OVALTINE SHAKE-UP! IT'S GOOD-TASTIN' AN' GOOD FOR YUH, TOO!

ORPHAN ANNIE AND SAN

LOOK!

Made of genuine Beetleware, this Little Orphan Annie Mug holds 8 full ounces—enough for a good big drink of ice-cold Ovaltine. (The actual mug is much bigger than this picture shows.) You'll have a barrel of fun with your Orphan Annie Shake-Up Mug this summer—so send the coupon right away.

During one of his periods of guardianship, "Daddy" took Annie and Joe on a yachting trip to the South Pacific. The crew rebelled for some obscure reason, setting Warbucks, Annie, and their friends off on an island equipped with an abandoned fort. Annie and her companions took refuge in the fort against the local natives, who stubbornly refused to recognize Warbucks as their master. The natives attacked the fort in which the party was trapped. Our heroes were armed with only a few automatic weapons and Little Orphan Annie's ingenuity, but it was enough.

Like most rugged individualists, Annie had many skills—including artistic talent. She drew a likeness of her own face—big circle for the head, two smaller circles for eyes, squiggles for hair. Over and over, she drew her own likeness. Big circle, two smaller circles, squiggles. Over and over. When she finished, she put one of these likenesses in each of the fort's gun ports. The natives moved closer and, thinking that the fort was manned by a veritable army of little red-headed girls, fled in panic like the ignorant savages they were.

The best news was yet to come. Annie was going to make a paper mask of her face available to every boy and girl listening at home. This was only one of several paper items Little Orphan Annie offered on her radio show. There was also a model circus with animated animals and clowns. Another item was Talking Stationery: when you opened the notepaper, a likeness of Annie moved its lips as if reading you the message on the paper. And it was the *Annie* radio show that made the decoding device badge popular. A new one was issued for each year, though between 1935 and 1940 the badges only differed from each other in slight respects, somewhat like the yearly models of automobiles.

However, a big change came for *Little Orphan Annie* in 1940. She lost her sponsor. It looked like Daddy Warbucks was dead for sure this time. "We may be down, but we ain't out," Annie said. Quaker Puffed Wheat ("Sparkies," as they called it then) picked up Annie's option for two more years, through 1942. They added something new as a replacement for Daddy Warbucks—Captain Sparks, a heroic young aviator. (The old sponsor, Ovaltine, had opted for the *Captain Midnight* series, whose hero was a mysterious aviator. If that was the sort of thing the kids wanted, Annie's show would get one, too. But Captain Sparks soon came to dominate the series, and Annie simply became the little girl sidekick, similar to Jane on *Tom Mix* or Joyce on *Captain Midnight.*)

The show offered a number of interesting premiums during this period. Some could be purchased in dime stores—like a water pistol, a camera, and a pocket flashlight—while others were made up specially for Annie: badges, secret manuals, code devices, a periscope, a silent dog whistle, a ring for spotting the altitude of airplanes from their apparent size.

My favorite premium from this period is the Little Orphan Annie Cockpit, more properly identified as the Orphan Annie-Captain Sparks Aviation Trainer, which consisted of a cardboard facsimile of an airplane's control board, rudder pedals, and a joy stick to steer by. The booklet that came with the set probably gave you all the information you would need to fly an airplane, but warned you sternly not to try to fly a *real* plane without aid from a live instructor.

Somewhere in the uncertain skies of 1942 Annie disappeared. What mystery lies behind her disappearance? Maybe she tried piloting with only the experience of her own training set under her belt. Like Amelia Earhart, some still search for her; some wait for her return. Where are you, Annie? The world needs your "sunny smile" and "host of healthfulness." Come back, Annie. We love you and miss you.

OTHERS BY LAND, SEA, BUT MOSTLY AIR

BUCK ROGERS

The second afternoon adventure serial to make it to network radio, after *Little Orphan Annie,* was *Buck Rogers* in 1932. Buck offered no 25th-century gear as representative as Annie's Shake-Up Mug, but all of his premiums are highly sought after and in general much more financially valuable than Annie's. Because he cuts across several fields of interest—science fiction, the comic strip, radio, movie serials, popular Americana—the resulting competition has tended to drive prices up.

One of the earliest radio offers—probably the first, although records are hazy—is a Solar Map of the planetary locations of some of Buck's adventures. There are also several Solar Scout handbooks and badges. Even the last premium of all, a glow-in-the dark crocodile band ring offered by Post Toasties during a short-lived revival of the program in 1945, is popular today. The ring differs from a Jack Armstrong ring only in that it has a red stone setting (Jack's was black).

Another time, *Terry and the Pirates* solicited your box tops for the ring with a green setting. (It was wartime and advertisers had to make do with what was available from manufacturers.) Those crocodiles started in the Sulu Sea, went to Saturn and Venus, and got back to Earth in China

TERRY AND THE PIRATES

Terry and the Pirates had the usual assortment of ring and badge offers, as well as portrait drawings of the characters by newspaper strip artist Milton Caniff. One of the premiums most favored by collectors is the Pirate Gold Detector Ring. When you look through what appears to be a tiny telescope set on a ring band, you can see a magnified view of a piece of real gold ore (so you will know what to look for if you are hunting a gold mine).

DICK TRACY

Another show of comic strip origin, *Dick Tracy,* offered many pieces of equipment for junior coppers. There was a huge pencil that wrote red on one end and blue on the other, with a cap that sounded like a siren when you blew through it. It would have been great for giving out traffic tickets: you could stop the cars with the siren and write out the ticket in either red or blue. At one period, Tracy got off on an aviation kick and offered more flying-oriented premiums than even Captain Midnight, including goggles, model planes, naval aviator's caps, etc. Also—as might be expected of a policeman—Dick Tracy had a real thing about badges. As a member of the Dick Tracy Secret Service Patrol, you could get a brass Rookie's badge, then a bronze Sergeant's badge, then a silver Lieutenant's, and finally a gold Captain's, each accompanied by appropriate certificates and handbooks.

I'm a bit uncertain about what you had to do to get this equipment, but I know a large part of it consisted of sending in various numbers of seals from Quaker Oats boxes. I vividly recall sending for some badge and weeks later receiving a personal letter—not a form letter, I'm sure—from a Quaker Oats company executive informing me that I was three box seals short of having enough for my badge. I could either send them those seals or, at my option, send them five cents in cold cash. I scraped up the money—which I found preferable to scraping a few dozen more bowls of oatmeal—and sent it on. In time, I did receive my badge. It couldn't have cost the company more than ten or twenty times the value of my nickel to solicit it. But I suppose that being connected with Dick Tracy made the men at Quaker Oats sticklers for rules and regulations.

SKY KING

After the end of World War Two, in the last days of radio drama, several new programs appeared and offered their own array of giveaways. Sky King took to the air right after V-J Day. He was described as a modern rancher who was a veteran of naval aviation. The exploits of Schuyler ("Sky") King seemed to be a combination of the successful elements of *Tom Mix* and *Captain Midnight*. When Sky's sponsor, Peter Pan Peanut Butter, got together with Jack Armstrong and Wheaties they pioneered a new format in afternoon children's serials. Instead of fifteen-minute serial installments, the two programs went to a series of complete-in-one-half-hour stories. Night-time mystery shows and the early evening *Lone Ranger* had used the format for decades, but so far only the quarter-hour serials had been employed in the afternoon. Initially, the two sponsors wanted to divide the time exactly evenly (buying no more than their established seventy-five minutes per week), so *Jack Armstrong* was heard three times (Monday, Wednesday, Friday) and *Sky King* twice (Tuesday and Thursday) the first week, with the order reversed the following week. Eventually, General Mills opted to buy fifteen minutes more of air time and *Jack Armstrong* became a Monday-Wednesday-Friday fixture with *Sky King* on the other two weekdays.

The new half-hour format was successful both commercially and dramatically. The thirty-minute stories were faster and more enjoyable than the old serials. Some really well-written shows such as Carlton Morse's *I Love a Mystery,* or even George Lowther's *Tom Mix,* could sustain an interest and anticipation which the discontinuous episode could not. But for the more routinely done shows such as *Sky King* the complete stories were more effective. (Very shortly, the thirty-minute format proved more effective for *Superman, Bobby Benson, Captain Midnight* and the rest.) At any rate, *Sky King's* pioneering change to the thirty-minute style soon brought all the competition into the same line, even including the venerable *Tom Mix.*

Sky King celebrated his success with an ample selection of premiums. He offered several glow-in-the-dark rings—one that just glowed, one that glowed and wrote secret messages with a tiny ball-point pen and then magnified them, and a third one that glowed and showed a picture of Sky in cowboy togs before changing magically to one of him in disguise as a stooped old man.

Still another ring had one luminous patch that could be clicked off and on in blinker fashion to send messages at night. Then the ring extended to a 3½-inch-long telescope so you could see the results of the message—enemy headquarters being blown off the face of the map by a direct hit. This was the largest ring ever offered by a radio program, too large to have actually been worn as a finger ring by anyone but the Jolly Green Giant. It was not the largest glow premium offered by Sky King, however. That distinction was claimed by the Signalscope, which had a luminous band for night signaling, a mirror to flash messages in sunlight, a whistle, and a magnifying glass. The code on the side offered simple signals for such messages as "Danger Ahead" and "Look Behind You."

STRAIGHT ARROW

While Sky King took to the air with Penny and Clipper, his niece and nephew, and old Jim Bell, Flying Crown ranch foreman, in Sky's plane, the *Songbird,* another fine-feathered radio friend was getting off the ground. Actually, Straight Arrow did not use feathers to fly but to decorate his Comanche headband. Straight Arrow was a sort of answer to all those who thought Tonto should have his own show. While he sometimes posed as rancher Steve Adams, the show made it clear that he was—I quote—"a full-blooded Comanche brave." His sidekick was an old Gabby Hayes type called Packy.

From his quiver, Straight Arrow pulled not just arrows but such premiums as a golden arrow-head (the counterpart of the Masked Man's silver bullet), a Trail Kit that fit on your wrist, a feathered headband, and a small tom-tom. The most sought-after premium from this series is a look-in ring showing a magnified picture of Straight Arrow—similar to the Tom Mix ring of a decade before—but now the picture was in full color and a photograph of the listener himself or herself (if supplied) was put inside the ring alongside the great Red Man himself.

SUPERMAN

There were many other radio serial heroes, but some seemed to be reluctant about offering premiums—at least ones unique to that show with the hero's name and likeness on them.

Superman may have been faster than a speeding bullet but he wasn't a whiz when it came to premiums. The best he had was a silver embossed ring with his likeness and the words "Superman Crusader's Ring." (His Crusaders stood for racial and religious equality. The story line hit the message pretty hard—never were there so many Catholic priests who knew how to use their dukes, so many Jews who were philanthropic baseball stars, so many black men who were a credit to their race.) This was the only radio box top write-in offer, to my knowledge, that had Superman's name and likeness on it. His face was on one of the several dozen Pep comic character buttons available in boxes of that cereal, but you did not have to send in for it.

At one time the show offered a copy of *Superman and the Flying Train,* a singing kiddie record, but this could be bought in stores and was not a specially tailored radio offer. At another time the program offered what purported to be a model of the rocket in which Superman came from the planet Krypton to Earth—but there was no identification to that effect on the model rocket.

THE GREEN HORNET

The Green Hornet seems to have offered only one ring, which had a reproduction of his famous seal. (You could also hide a nickel inside the huge secret compartment.)

The ring was a copy of the one Brit Reid would use to imprint his Hornet seal on the forehead of a racketeer who had felt the power of the masked avenger's gas gun. Then Reid would fade into the night to meet faithful Kato at the Black Beauty super-car and return to the publisher's office at the *Daily Sentinel.*

Your own Green Hornet seal ring was best used for imprinting your Big Red pencil tablet and carrying money for a Baby Ruth.

SERGEANT PRESTON OF THE YUKON

Sergeant Preston of the Yukon got into the act fairly late. The show had been around for years, but in the late forties Quaker Puffed Wheat picked it up to replace the serialized *Terry and the Pirates* when the complete-in-one-episode format became popular. (The sponsor wisely went to George Trendle's WXYZ, which had developed that format so expertly for *The Lone Ranger.*) The fearless Mountie offered a reproduction of his famous police whistle complete with his signature, just like the one he had often used to summon his great lead dog, Yukon King. He also let us in on how he first became a mounted policeman and how he found his wonder dog. These stories ap-

peared in small comic books that came inside packages of Quaker Puffed Wheat and Rice, and the tales were dramatized on phonograph records which you could get for a quarter each and a box top. (These were special editions of ones also offered in stores.) Looking back on it, this was probably the ideal radio premium: a sample of the radio show itself.

But the good Sergeant let us down. One of his offerings was a deed to one square inch of Yukon gold territory, held by the Yukon Big Inch Land Co. Recently, collector Gerry Kramer investigated and found that those deeds are no longer valid. I had expected Sergeant Preston to stand behind those deeds in perpetuity.

Many other shows—*Hop Harrigan, Tennessee Jed, Jimmy Allen, The Sea Hound* (remember Captain Silver?), *Bobby Benson* among them—offered rings and badges and more, but never with the open-handed abandon of the leaders. In fact, several shows offered virtually the same premium—*Tennessee Jed* (who always got his man "daid center") had a "lookaround" ring with a mirror for peeking around corners which was almost identical to the one offered by Tom Mix. Then the siren-whistle ring device used by Tom Mix was also employed in rings offered by Dick Tracy and Captain Midnight. Apparently there are only so many viable ideas for premiums. You still see some of the same concepts popping up today, usually offered right in the cereal box: decoder rings, telescopes, microscopes, model planes, etc.

The old original radio premiums mentioned above sell for a wide variety of prices, depending on the personal opinion of the buyer and seller. Ten dollars would seem to be rock bottom in collectors' circles, while a hundred dollars or more is sometimes paid for the rarest and most desired items. The best advice to any would-be collector is to pay only what the item is worth to you.

LOVELY, DELIGHTFUL RADIO PREMIUMS TOUCHED WITH MOONGLOW AND DAWN

Believe it or not, there were *some* radio premiums I heard constantly advertised that I had no interest in sending for. A Tom Mix ring that enabled you to look around corners to see if espionage agents lay in wait—now, that was something worth your Ralston box top and 10¢ in coin. But who would want a Helen Trent Friendship Locket that was patterned after an early Colonial design and which was thought to bring happiness in married romance to all who wore it? Not me.

But a few million housewives and possibly some young girls who listened to soap operas must have sent for such things. These other premiums were as persuasively sold as the ones on the kids' serials. The show would go something like this:

GIL: Helen. . . Helen. . . your face is as lovely this evening as your own Friendship Locket.

HELEN: Gil, you'll turn my head. Few things are as lovely as this original Colonial design I discovered on my trip back East with Roger Blakewell.

GIL: Roger Blakewell, the handsome but insane Broadway producer?

HELEN: Gil, let's not speak of Roger Blakewell tonight. His plan for selling out America's Panama defenses is forever ended. His chorus girl accomplices have all gone before the firing squad and he will spend the rest of his days in a straitjacket.

GIL: Yes, we can be thankful that the American stage is safe from his foreign influence. You're right. We'll say no more of Roger Blakewell. Ah, why do handsomeness and insanity so often go hand in hand? But no more. Helen, tonight let us speak only of. . . us. . . and your lovely Friendship Locket that reflects your own beauty.

HELEN: Perhaps, Gil, it is only I who reflect the beauty of the Friendship Locket. Oh listen, Gil, I think I heard Agatha come in with her worn, old, black shawl.

AGATHA: Why, land sakes, I didn't know you two young people were in here by the crackling fire. I'll just say hello and go on up to my room in the back of Helen's spacious house.

GIL: Sit down, Agatha, and have a cup of coffee with us. Why, I see Helen has given you one of her own Friendship Lockets. Its tasteful blend of colors goes well with your silver hair.

AGATHA: Thank you, Gil. Yes, the Friendship Locket is the nicest present I've ever had in my seventy-five years of life. I'd gladly kill to get one, if I didn't have it.

HELEN: Coffee, Agatha dear?

AGATHA: Helen. . . I wasn't going to tell you this tonight. . . so you could get at least one more good night's sleep in this life. . .

HELEN: There's something wrong. I sense it. Tell me, Agatha.

AGATHA: I'd give anything if I didn't have to tell you—even my Friendship Locket—but tell you I must. Eastern big-city doctors have released the insane Broadway producer, Roger Blakewell!

ANNOUNCER: Helen's face drains of blood, as Gil crushes a coffee cup in his strong, masculine hand. Have Eastern big-city doctors actually released the handsome but insane producer who has vowed to blow up the Panama Canal and who has told Helen he will have her or no man will? Tune in tomorrow to find out. . . AND. . . to hear the first announcement about a new gift. . . something that Helen wants to send to you personally. Can you guess what it is?

I could guess.

The costume jewelry could hardly interest me as a boy, but in recent years I've begun to collect all sorts of radio memorabilia and have discovered that other shows besides the adventure serials had their own giveaways.

Maps: A number of shows gave away maps of their fictional territories. Of course there was a Little Orphan Annie map of Simmons Corners and a Jack Armstrong Treasure Map (at least two, in fact), but there was also a Lum and Abner map of Pine Ridge and an Amos 'n' Andy chart of Weber City (where they resided before moving to the big city).

Flower Seeds: Giving away seeds to start a home garden seemed to be a popular idea. At various times, *Ma Perkins, David Harum, Stella Dallas,* and even *I Love a Mystery* went to seeds.

Cookbooks: Aunt Jenny had one to tell you how to prepare all sorts of delicious goodies with her favorite shortening, Spry. It had several photos of Aunt Jenny herself. Other programs often offered cookbooks, especially if their sponsor was a food product, but they did not always have a name or likeness from the radio program itself.

The best of the cookbooks was from *One Man's Family.* It offered Fanny Barbour's favorite recipes as a twentieth anniversary gift. One might be momentarily taken aback by Fanny and Henry Barbour celebrating their twentieth anniversary, since they had grown children well into their forties by this time, but they were celebrating the twentieth year of their radio series, created and produced by Carlton E. Morse.

Fanny's cookbook abounded with photos of all the family members, dating back decades in some cases. Since the cast remained essentially the same for all those years, the family portraits did show the same person aging gracefully over a span of years.

Actually, this cookbook was only one of a number of giveaways from *One Man's Family*—others were made to look like a family album, a diary, a scrapbook, etc. In them you could see Paul Barbour (portrayed by Michael Raffetto) as a dark-haired pilot still sulking about World War One in 1932, and then Paul as a gray-haired airline executive in 1952. The same pages offered shots of Jack Barbour (Page Gillman) growing from a young boy to a young man. Mother and Father Barbour, Fanny and Henry (Minnetta Ellen and J. Anthony Smythe) are omnipresent.

There had to be some deft editing of the photographs in some cases. Katherine Wilson retired from the role of Claudia Barbour to be replaced in later years by Barbara Fuller. The blonde Barbara resembled the brunette Katherine not in the least. New heads of Barbara were pasted in on old group shots. There were also some cast changes concerning Claudia's husband, Nickie. In the final years of the show, the shift of actors became almost universal, with only the original Father Barbour and son Jack remaining. (Bernice Berwin as Hazel Barbour was still receiving credit on the show, but had in fact left the cast and had not yet been replaced.) Publicity releases for the radio show now had to be content with current family portraits, since the old photographs of Barbour history would no longer match up.

In all, *One Man's Family* offered many souvenir booklets. Fans of Carlton Morse's other great night-time show, *I Love a Mystery,* have often asked me if that series ever offered any premiums. Well, there was the flower seeds offer previously mentioned, and one item directly connected with the broadcast—a glossy photograph of Jack, Doc, and Reggie getting ready to go into action. And what action—the three soldiers of fortune carrying a hypnotized Chinese girl across the country with every crook and killer alive out to stop them. Then in a later adventure, Jack and Doc alone climbing "The Stairway to the Sun" to the lost plateau of prehistoric monsters and an ancient Higher Intelligence that guided the destiny of mankind. Dinosaurs, werewolves, a Temple of Vampires, they tackled them all. The Three Comrades were too grown-up to offer decoder rings, but a photo album of their adventures would sure have been a great

thing to have. My interest in such an *I Love a Mystery* premium would have been directly proportional to my lack of interest in having a Helen Trent Friendship Locket. In those days, the full moon suggested less boy-girl romance to me than the excitement of the eerie howling of a werewolf. I just wasn't cut out for the finer things.

MAGAZINES

COLLECTING MAGAZINES FOR FUN—
AND PROFIT

We all read comic books as kids. The colored pages of cloaked and masked figures fascinated us by allowing escape into a world where we could be all-powerful, from a world where we were totally without power—pushed around by parents, schoolteachers and bullies, laid low by constant colds, the measles and assorted maladies.

Comics, of course, were not our only escape—mystery and adventure abounded on the radio and in the movie theaters, and even in books and magazines with more text than pictures. To some of us, the other media were more important than comics—for me, it was radio. While there were scores of shows that I simply could not allow myself to miss—*Tom Mix, Jack Armstrong, Superman, Captain Midnight* in the afternoon, *The Lone Ranger* a bit later, and *I Love a Mystery, The Hermit's Cave,* and *Inner Sanctum* in the evening, there were only a couple of comic books (*Captain Marvel* and *All-Star Comics* featuring the Justice Society) that I always made a point of picking up. Mostly, I was a dilettante where comics were concerned, only buying issues of special appeal, such as ones featuring a particularly interesting villain like Captain Marvel Jr.'s foe, Captain Nazi, or first issues with "origin stories" of how the hero "got that way," or "book-length" stories where the whole magazine was devoted to a single adventure instead of having three or four individual tales about the hero. (Now virtually all comic magazines have only one long story about a continuing hero, but aside from advertising pages, the story itself may run no more than 18 pages—about the same length as one of the several stories in the old 64-page comics.)

As I grew older, the ragged-edged pulps like *Startling Stories, Thrilling Wonder Stories* and *Black Book Detective* (featuring a competitor to The Shadow called the Black Bat) attracted more of my enthusiastic interest than comic books. But still the comic books were always there. You picked up one here and there, sticking by a few old favorites, until you finally left them—or until those favorites went out of business, like Captain Marvel, and left you.

Lately I have become a comic book collector. A newspaper reporter recently interviewed a teenage collector. "Comic collecting is like taking drugs," the young man said. "You start out just sort of playing around with some cheap stuff, but before long you are going after harder and harder stuff, getting into big money."

And old comic books can be worth big money. There has been so much publicity in national news magazines, on television, and in the papers that now most people are well aware of the fact. Indeed, some people have developed distorted ideas. They think that one of the last *Little Orphan Annie* Big Little Books from 1949 should be worth fifty dollars. (It's really only worth about two dollars.) At the same time, the average person often does not realize quite how valuable old comic books can be. A few years ago a dealer negotiated the purchase of a stack of old comics from a grandmotherly type in the Midwest. The old lady cannily demanded *one thousand dollars* for the stack of a hundred or so old comics. She got it. But within days the dealer had over half of his money back from the sale of only *two* comics out of that hundred—*Detective Comics* No. 27 and *Action Comics* No. 1, with the first appearances of Batman and Superman, respectively. Now the dealer could realize *more* than that thousand dollars from the sale of those two magazines.

One major period in comic book collecting—probably the most active one—has virtually come to an end. That is the one which involved lucking onto a trove of old comics in some attic, basement, trunk or closet and then cheating the owner, in the best American tradition of horse trading, out of them with a few dollars.

"Cheating" is possibly too strong a term (though possibly not). Sometimes it is simply a matter of the books' being worth a great deal more to the collector than to the original owner. And of course it might have taken the original owner a long time to sell off each copy, one by one, for a potentially greater sum than the collector offered in one bulk purchase. Since I have never had the golden opportunity of relieving an elderly widow of a huge pile of comics for a couple of bucks, I cannot say how fair an offer I would make her, but I do know many collectors are motivated by the most cynical greed imaginable—and gloat for years over the success of their con jobs.

There are very few attics remaining to be tapped. A major new find in comic books has not been made for three or four years. By the law of averages, there must still be some mothers who have not yet thrown out the treasures of their now middle-aged sons, but they are a rare breed. Mothers always seem to have an irresistible compulsion to throw out stacks of old comics or boxes full of old rings and badges from radio shows. Broken lamps and useless furniture can clutter attics and garages for decades, but let a son turn his back—go off to college, or into the army, or even go on a camping trip for a few weeks—and out goes the priceless junk into the ashcan.

If all the attics have have been picked clean of *Captain America* and *Wonder Woman,* then all the old comic books left must be in the hands of collectors or dealers who realize their potential cash value. That is, in fact, the situation. Comic collecting now has many of the aspects of coin and stamp collecting. When comic books change hands these days, it is generally for close to full market value. They are bought for the personal pleasure of adding to one's collection—often to complete a run, most of which was gathered at a lower price in years past—or in the expectation that prices will rise even further and that, like many investments, the old comic will accrue in value. At any rate, the present state of comic collecting requires someone not only with a more than casual interest in the subject, but with the ability to invest hundreds of dollars quite regularly in his hobby.

I fear that as a collector I have always been a ragpicker. In years past, I thrived on going around to old book shops, Salvation Army stores and the like, picking up the items that were only junk to the storekeepers but were treasures to me. No doubt my attitude was similar to that of the speculators who now chortle over cleaning some little old lady out of three thousand dollars' worth of comics for five bucks. But the difference in

price was slight in those days and it was the thrill of the game that engaged me (to be able to get a copy of *The Shadow* for a dime, when I knew it was worth at least seventy-five cents, was a triumph).

It was difficult to feel much sympathy for the book dealers you outwitted. For one thing, a large majority of them seemed to be nastily insane. Having given their dispositions some thought, I've come to the conclusion that since they usually bought the old magazines for a few cents a *pound,* they had only contempt for the fools who would actually pay one or two dollars for a book for which they paid a fraction of a cent. Also, book store owners often delighted in bullying and insulting their customers, who would take it and come back for more just to get those old *Doc Savage* or *Amazing Stories* or *Batman* magazines. In some cases their hostility even exceeded their greed (certainly a milestone of accomplishment); some of them actually came to prefer insulting and thwarting their customers to making a sale.

To give an example, a friend told me of spotting an article on *The Lone Ranger* radio show in an old *Radio Mirror* magazine which was mixed in with movie magazines like *Photoplay* at a certain book store. Being interested in the radio article myself, I went to the book store and told the counterman I wanted to buy that radio magazine. "We got no radio mags," he told me. "I understand a few got mixed in with your movie magazines by mistake," I replied. The man literally snarled. "We don't make no mistakes here! Get out!"

A few months later I came back for more (such is the curse of the collector). At that time, I bought about twenty copies of *Spicy Western* from a pile of magazines he considered worthless junk. They cost me thirty cents a copy, but I could have resold them at ten dollars a copy. I must admit I had no qualms about taking advantage of that particular book dealer. The Shadow isn't the only one to taste the sweetness of Revenge.

Book store browsing is itself a thing of nostalgia. Today, even the most ignorant used book store manager is aware that old comic books and pulp magazines are worth money. Those warehouses where they once found such old magazines for a few cents a pound twenty years ago are now empty. If some old issue finds its way into their hands, traded in by some unaware customer, the dealer usually overestimates the value. I remember going through a sleazy skid-row book store—one of my regular haunts—only a few months ago and seeing an old *Mad* from the era when it was in comic book form. It was tattered and falling apart, but the dealer had scrawled across the cover in black marking pen, $14.00. That price mark alone so defaced the magazine that it would cut whatever value it had in half. Any book or magazine of the slightest interest is now usually marked up to the absolute top price anyone would ever pay for it.

Virtually all volunteer service organization thrift shops have all their books and magazines culled by professional dealers before they place them on sale—often in violation of announced policy. So bargains are seldom to be found there.

The sanest way to collect old comics or other old magazines today is to deal with established dealers with a large stock. Although really low prices are long gone, relatively low prices are sometimes obtained by settling for secondary condition—getting a slightly battered copy of *Superman* No. 9 for ten dollars, for instance, rather than a mint copy for thirty-five dollars—or very occasionally by finding a dealer who is overstocked. If by some strange turn of chance the dealer happens to have located a stack of thirty copies of *Green Lantern* No. 17, he will probably quote a low price of four dollars for that issue, rather than the twelve dollars a dealer might charge if he only had one copy on hand. Such a thing is becoming rarer and rarer, but only a few months ago one dealer uncovered a warehouse full of *Tip Top Comics* and was selling his hundreds of copies at only a quarter of the usual price.

Collecting old magazines is fun in itself. And if the collector can keep from being obsessed with sheer acquisitive greed, he can take great pleasure in the rewards of the game.

COMICS

COMIC BOOKS

My love of comic books as a boy was really part of my love for books in general. I regarded those brightly illustrated magazines as books, and the ever-growing stack of them was part of my library.

Those adults still interested in comics today are often oriented toward art and illustration; as kids, they loved movies, the Sunday comics, and comic books. So did I, but I also avidly read pulp magazines and hardcover novels and listened to radio's word pictures. In short, I loved a good story—in any form.

The first comic magazines I ever saw were tattered, coverless copies left by some kid in my uncle's grocery store. (I remember the event so vividly that some will doubt my credibility, but then a person who writes books on nostalgia is hardly normal.) One of these, I now know, was *Whiz Comics* No. 4, dated May 1940. It concerned Billy Batson's encounter with the wicked scientist Dr. Sivana, who used a ray on young Billy to rob him of his memory, including the knowledge that he could change into mighty Captain Marvel merely by saying the magic word, Shazam.

With the accidental good fortune of so many comic book characters, Billy wandered dazedly down an abandoned subway tunnel where he had first been granted his powers by an old wizard some months before. Seeing the magician's name on the wall, he spoke it: "Shazam!" In a flash of enchanted lightning he once again was the World's Mightiest Mortal, Captain Marvel, able to defeat the plans of the fiendish little scientist.

Another of my first comic books was (I now know) a copy of *Slam Bang Comics.* I've never been able to find out what issue it was, but I recall a story of Zoro the Mystery Man (a city-dwelling relative of Old California's Zorro, perhaps). In this story, Zoro was fighting some gangsters armed with revolvers and automatics using only his sword cane. He taunted them, "Cold steel in my hands is better than hot lead in yours!" I admired the play on words, and have remembered it for some thirty years.

A third was a battered copy of *Marvel Mystery Comics* with Human Torch and Sub-Mariner stories, which didn't leave particularly lasting impressions on me. Another feature in the back of the book puzzled me because at first glance it seemed to star Superman—except that he had a mustache. It was actually another character known as The Angel, who bore only a superficial resemblance to the Man of Steel, but what does a dumb kid know?

Yes, I knew who Superman was—even though these were the first comic books I had ever seen—for the big-city paper that came to our town, the *St. Louis Post-Dispatch,* carried Superman in the daily and Sunday funnies. From these newspaper strips I had developed some standards of judgment; to me, Superman seemed far better than the blue-suited Angel or the other sloppily drawn characters in *Marvel Mystery*. Zoro the Mystery Man seemed to me then to be almost as good as Superman, though, and the story of little Billy who could change into big Captain Marvel struck me as even better.

I'm sure the first comic book I ever *bought* off the stands was an issue of Superman. I think it was the sixth issue, which has an autographed picture of Superman on the cover. It looked like something to *save*. (I had not yet gotten around to saving the Sunday funnies.)

The dam had burst. Comic books were flooding down on me. Among the earliest comic books I bought were *All-Star Comics* No. 5 with only the third meeting of the elder gods of Comic-book-land, the Justice Society of America (Hawkman, Green Lantern, Flash, The Spectre, and others, all in one club, one story); *World's Finest Comics* No. 2 with separate stories of both Superman and Batman; *More Fun Comics* No. 66 with a feature-length story of the ghostly Spectre, and many, many others.

In the fifties there was a lot of agitation about the trashiness of comic books and their evil influence on kids. But in the forties in the middle-class Middle West comic books were accepted as just another fun part of childhood like roller skates, ice cream cones, and fireworks on the Fourth of July. The only objections I had from my parents about comic books was what it was costing them to keep me supplied.

But while I loved and saved my comic books, I was never exclusively obsessed with them. I kept on reading anything that I could get my hands on—*Lone Eagle* pulp magazines, *Weird Tales,* A. Merritt's novel, *Seven Footprints to Satan,* the Sherlock Holmes tales, and so on.

Even after I had gotten deep into the world of science fiction via *Thrilling Wonder Stories* and *Startling Stories* I never abandoned comic books completely. I read them through World War Two, when most of them deteriorated badly, shrunk to half their page count by paper rationing and illustrated by second-rate "artists" who somehow escaped the draft.

When the E.C. line started with such titles as *Weird Science* and *Weird Fantasy* about 1950 I was ripe for their horror and science fiction. *Mad's* irreverent humor spoke to me as it did to so many others. When censorship by pressure groups forced *Mad* (and its competitors) out of existence, when the Justice Society was disbanded in *All-Star,* when Captain Marvel was forced into retirement in the early fifties, I gave up comic books. It wasn't that I had outgrown them; it was just that all my favorites had gone out of business for various reasons.

Around 1960 many old titles began reappearing —new models of *The Flash, Green Lantern,* and a slightly refurbished version of the Justice Society— *The Justice League of America*. I began buying these for old times' sake. When the first issue of *Fantastic Four* appeared, I got that because it had The Human Torch, another remodeled forties character, in the group. I bought many of these DC and Marvel comic books because they revived the Golden Age of superheroes, and because I was interested in seeing their growth of maturity and sophistication. The growth finally seemed to reach a plateau and level off. The plane was higher in the forties but not at a level of truly mature artistic expression. Perhaps the magazines could not go higher and still be recognizably comic books.

I think I know where comic books are at today, and I know where they come from. Even when I was looking at those beat-up funny books in my uncle's store, I knew there was only one guy who belonged in long blue underwear.

SUPERMAN

It was the Man of Steel with powers far beyond those of ordinary men—the man from another world, the strange planet called Krypton—who made comic magazines a national phenomenon. His was the first success story of a new industry.

Newspaper reprints had been around since the first issue of *Famous Funnies* in 1934 (and even a few trial issues before that). All-original comic magazines like *Fun Comics* (later *More Fun)* appeared in 1935, and comic books with central themes like *Detective Comics* were available in 1937. But the genre waited until the creation of Superman in the first issue of *Action Comics* in June, 1938, before there was a real hit.

Two men still in their teens, Jerry Siegel and Joe Shuster, created this legend. The actual moment of inspiration had come years before the first publication. It was a steamy hot night in the summer of 1933 in Cleveland, Ohio. Seventeen-year-old Jerry Siegel lay on clammy bed sheets looking out his window at clouds drifting across the face of the yellow moon. If only he could get away from the heat, rise above everything, fly out past the moon . . . In that thought, Superman was born.

Creation did not come in an instant flash, but, as Jim Steranko tells it in his *History of Comics,* Volume I, young Siegel lay awake the rest of the night, building his creature bit by bit. "I hop right out of bed and write this down, and then I go back and think some more for about two hours and get up again . . . This goes on all night . . . until in the morning I have a complete script."

With the light of dawn, Siegel walked twelve blocks to the home of his friend Joe Shuster. He explained his new character with all the enthusiasm of youth, and Shuster was caught up in the dream. Feverishly he began to sketch out drawings of what this Superman would look like.

Originally, Superman owed a lot to previous fictional characters. In his physical and mental superiority, he resembled Doc Savage, the pulp hero sometimes referred to as a "superman." (The word was not new. Scientists and philosophers had

theorized about a superman or race of supermen for centuries.) In his skintight acrobat's costume, he was preceded by Lee Falk's newspaper comic strip hero, The Phantom. His double identity could be traced back to Johnston McCulley's Zorro, or the Red Shadow of the Romberg-Hammerstein operetta, *Desert Song,* or even before. There had been visitors from other planets in science fiction for dozens of years, many of them having superhuman powers of one sort or another. But never before had all these elements been put together in quite this magical way.

The normal course of development for significant fictional creations is a series of experiments that finally produce a winner. But Superman was the first of his kind and a smash success. The characters who went before him expressed only one aspect of his total image. Sherlock Holmes was preceded by Dupin and Nick Carter, for example, but the Man of Steel was born full-blown.

The origin of Superman—in *Action Comics* No. 1, June, 1938—was explained thus: "Just before the doomed planet Krypton exploded to fragments, a scientist placed his infant son within an experimental rocket-ship, launching it toward Earth . . . [Rescued from the burning rocket and later adopted] by an elderly couple, the Kents, [young Clark Kent] learned to his delight that he could hurdle skyscrapers . . . leap an eighth of a mile . . . raise tremendous weights . . . run faster than a streamline train . . . and nothing less than a bursting shell could penetrate his skin!"

The first issue of *Action* showing Superman lifting the "tremendous weight" of an automobile over his head sold out, and was in fact reprinted three times by the publishers. Yet today there are only approximately twelve complete copies of that issue known to exist. One recently changed hands for a reported $1,800. The event made headlines in newspapers around the country and at the moment is a record price for any single comic magazine. Other copies of *Action Comics* No. 1 have sold for four hundred to six hundred dollars in recent years and may do so again.

Remarkably enough, the publishers of *Action,* Detective Comics, Inc. (named after one of their earliest magazines) couldn't account for the sudden leap in their sales figures. Was it the magician,

Zatara? Adventurer Clip Carson? Sports champion Pep Morgan? Or Superman? Since Superman was the only new character in the line-up, the answer now seems obvious. Magicians and civilian detectives had been running through the pages of *More Fun, Adventure,* and *Detective Comics* for several years. Siegel and Shuster had even contributed such plainclothes sleuths as *Slam Bradley* and *Federal Men.* But Superman was the important ingredient. After experimenting with covers that did not feature Superman and did not sell as well, the publishers got the idea. By the summer of 1939, Superman was also featured in a magazine devoted exclusively to his exploits. The first issue of *Superman* reprints the single Man of Steel stories from the first four numbers of *Action* and is only a shade less valuable than the first *Action* (the record price for it so far is $1,000).

Superman subsequently appeared in many other comics, such as *New York World's Fair Comics* (which became *World's Best,* then *World's Finest*), *All-Star Comics,* and, later, *Justice League of America* (and even others); in hundreds of newspaper comic sections; in animated and live-action movies; on radio and television; and merchandised on all types of games, clothing and toys—Superman belts, Superman wallets, a Superman Krypto Ray Gun which projected a "movie" on the wall. The comic magazines also started the Supermen of America, offering a four-color pin-back button, a secret code chart and certificate of membership which drew millions of fans. The latest development is a Disneyland-type amusement park being built at Metropolis, Illinois. If nothing else, Superman is a super businessman.

A vast industry—not just Superman, but the whole comic book business—sprang from an idea had by "two small, shy, nervous, myopic lads," as they have been described. Jerry Siegel and Joe Shuster made their hero everything they wished to be and were not—muscular, confident, cool, with X-ray vision. And much more. Superman acted out their fantasies of instant justice over bullying tormentors—fantasies entertained by virtually every human being at one time or another.

In the earliest stories, the Man of Steel would smash the presses of lying newspapers (not his *Daily Planet,* of course) and would use his super-strength to hurl a crooked used-car salesman off the Earth and out beyond the orbit of Pluto. But soon pressure groups tamed Superman down to a goody-goody guy who helped little old ladies cross the ocean, although he could still get a bit nasty with the Nazis and some fiendish crooks like the mad scientist Lothar. Enough of Siegel and Shuster's original wish-fulfillment survived so that Superman survived and prospered.

Siegel and Shuster did not do too badly themselves. In 1940, *The Saturday Evening Post* reported their gross earnings at $75,000 (easily worth a quarter of a million today). However, they had sold "all rights" to the publisher for the two hundred dollars they had received for the original story. Countless trips to court have failed to change that. Many harsh things have been said—as, for instance, when the publishers fired cartoonist Joe Shuster after he started to go blind. Given the opportunity, they probably would have fired the crippled newsboy of the comics, Freddy Freeman.

After the departure of Siegel and Shuster, *Superman* was controlled by editor Mort Weissinger. Confidently, Weissinger changed virtually everything about the successful character, adding and subtracting powers, inventing a new origin and a vast and confusing family for the erstwhile "sole survivor" of Krypton. But even these "improvements" couldn't kill the character. Superman could indeed survive anything. Today, the Man of Steel is managed by Julius Schwartz (under the supervision of editorial director Carmine Infantino). Schwartz has cut back the character to his original size and improved the feature over the Weissinger era. One of the greatest of all comics editors, Schwartz is probably responsible for the survival of the comic magazine format into the seventies by his reintroduction of streamlined superheroes in the late fifties. All the other escapist publishing formats of the thirties have vanished—the pulp magazine, the Big Little Book, even the major weekly picture magazine. But comic books keep chugging down the track, thanks to men like Julie Schwartz.

BATMAN

The success of Superman inspired countless imitations, two of which were destined for tremendous success. Less than a year after Superman appeared, the same company introduced another new character in an established magazine. *Detective Comics* No. 27 of May, 1939, offered the first appearance of Batman. The cover shows him swinging across a rooftop on a rope, dragging a struggling gunman with him.

Less original in concept than Superman, Bob Kane's Batman was more of an adaptation of the pulp magazine's Shadow for comic books. The new character wore a skintight acrobat's costume, somewhat like Superman's, but he skulked in the gloomy darkness like The Shadow, preying on fear-crazed crooks. The surprise ending of the first story is now familiar: "Bruce Wayne returns home to his room . . . a little later his door slowly opens . . . and reveals its occupant . . . if the commissioner could see his young friend now . . . he'd be amazed to learn that he is the 'Bat-Man'!"

Most collectors think these very early stories in *Detective* Nos. 27 through 37 are the best Batman tales of all. Though done in Kane's simplistic, wooden style (the very soul of "comic book"), they show a weirdly mysterious avenger, not above gunning down his enemies. Issue No. 33 revealed his "origin" story and the reason for his crusade. As a boy, Bruce Wayne had seen his parents die at the hands of a gangster. On their graves, Bruce swore to "avenge their deaths by spending the rest of my life warring on all criminals." Later, as a man, after years of physical and mental training, he mused: "I must be a creature of the night. Black, terrible . . . a . . . a . . ." Suddenly, a bat, confusedly darting about city streets, flew in the window. "A bat! That's it! It's an omen . . . I shall become a BAT!"

The change in Batman came in *Detective* No. 38 with the introduction of Dick Grayson, known as Robin, the Boy Wonder. Dick's parents were also murdered by gangland killers, and Bruce Wayne had taken him under his bat-wing, adopting him and teaching him how to fight armed thugs twice his size and age. The introduction of this new bird, with his Robin-red vest and laughing boy's face, changed the character of the strip, making it much less grim. Though changed, the feature remained tremendously successful, inspiring countless boy sidekicks: The Shield's Dusty, Mr. Scarlet's Pinky, Sandman's Sandy, *et al.*

Together, Batman and Robin battled the killer clown, the Joker, the pompous Penguin, the monstrous Two-Face. and many others in *Detective, Batman,* and *World's Finest Comics,* and in most of the other media that Superman appeared in.

Superman DC Publications, as they finally came to call themselves, seemed to have the superhero market really sewed up with their two tremendous hits, Superman and Batman, and with a skyful of lesser but charismatic characters: Sandman (who put crooks to sleep with his gas gun, and in later stories invaded their dreams); Hourman (who had one hour of super-strength after taking a Miraculo pill); Starman (who flew with an astral rod wand, charged by starlight); Hawkman (who had artificial wings and who could speak the language of the birds); The Flash (Fastest Man Alive, due to an exposure to radioactive chemicals that speeded up his life processes); Green Lantern (using a magic ring whose rays responded to his will power in miraculous ways); The Spectre (a living dead man, a ghost with powers almost equal to those of God Himself); Dr. Fate (a helmeted mortal somewhat like The Spectre); and many, many others.

No one company in the comics field has had such a great array of characters. Though some have been discontinued, they are still revived from time to time, and their exploits are constantly reprinted in comic books and in hardcover format. Finally, DC added Wonder Woman, a wonderfully eccentric strip with a life of its own. All these characters formed their own club, The Justice Society, in *All-Star Comics.* It seemed as if DC had everything.

Well, not quite everything.

SPECIAL EDITION COMICS

NUMBER ONE

64 PAGES—NEW ADVENTURES OF

CAPTAIN MARVEL

A FAWCETT PUBLICATION

10¢

Featuring
Brand-New Stories of
CAPTAIN MARVEL
World's Mightiest Man

WORLD'S MIGHTIEST FUNNY BOOK

Fawcett Publications had Captain Marvel.

Captain Marvel was an imitation of Superman, but roughly in the way that Woody Allen is an imitation of Bogart. Or, perhaps more accurately, in the way James Garner is an imitation of Tom Mix. The World's Mightiest Mortal, Captain Marvel, was heroic, but he was also funny—the warmest, most human of all the superhumans.

The Captain first showed up on the cover of *Whiz Comics* in February, 1940. As Superman had done for his first appearance, Captain Marvel was lifting an automobile—in fact, throwing it! He wore a crimson military outfit, like something out of a 19th-century operetta—an off-the-shoulder embroidered cape with sash and boots. Originally he wore a jacket with a button-down shoulder flap, but this shrunk after a few issues to a tight-fitting one-piece shirt. Always, of course, the lightning bolt emblem was there on his chest.

Captain Marvel's "origin" tale was simple, childishly simple. A poor newsboy, Billy Batson, was lured down into a deserted subway tunnel, where he saw an ancient, white-bearded man standing before an awesome throne.

"Welcome, Billy Batson!" the Old One intoned.

"H-how did you know my name?" Billy asked.

"I know everything! I am—SHAZAM . . . All my life I have fought injustice and cruelty! But I am old now—and my time is almost up! You shall be my successor! Merely by speaking my name, you can become the strongest and mightiest man in the world—CAPTAIN MARVEL! Speak my name!

"Shazam!" Billy managed in astonishment.

In a stroke of magic lightning, Billy became Captain Marvel. Despite the fantastic change, the fundamental but ingenious drawing style showed us that although Billy had been changed drastically, he was still basically the same person. He was taller and more muscular, a well-developed grown man with his tousled, boyish hair smoothed into neat waves. His red sweater and blue slacks had been replaced by the gold-trimmed crimson uniform the world would come to know. He was now the World's Mightiest Mortal, gifted with the powers of six ancient heroes (five Greek, one Jewish). They were:

> Solomon (Wisdom)
> Hercules (Strength)
> Atlas (Stamina)
> Zeus (Power)
> Achilles (Courage)
> Mercury (Speed)

Old Shazam then used more of his magic to conjure up the Historama, a color console TV (a good trick in 1940). The screen reviewed for Billy what he well knew—how his crooked uncle had cheated him out of his parents' legacy and forced him out onto the street to peddle his papers. But he had been good and the old wizard had rewarded him with more physical power than any other mortal had ever held. It was enough to make you want to follow the Boy Scout oath to the letter.

Dazedly, back in his own youthful form, Billy wandered down the subway tunnel past the statues of the Seven Deadly Enemies of Man (Pride, Envy, Greed, Hatred, Selfishness, Laziness, Injustice) and went out into the nighttime street.

The next day, a headline in one of his own papers told him of the work of a nutty scientist, one who vowed to drive all radio stations off the air unless he was paid five million dollars. Changing to Captain Marvel, our hero decided to put a stop to this. He wrecked the madman's plan, battered some of his hoods pretty badly, and smashed the TV set on which he saw the leering face of the World's Wickedest Scientist, Sivana!

WE INTERRUPT THIS ACCOUNT FOR A SPECIAL BULLETIN!

For the first time anywhere, I can reveal a new element to the origin of Captain Marvel. Our hero (Captain/Billy) should have realized he had seen that same face on a TV screen twice within a few days. Comparing the faces of Billy's uncle, the old skinflint, and Dr. Sivana, the little fiend, we can see that they are virtually the same!

FOR THE FIRST TIME, THE AMAZING MAGIC LIGHTNING THUNDERS DOWN!

BOOM

AND FOR THE FIRST TIME IN HISTORY, CAPTAIN MARVEL, THE WORLD'S MIGHTIEST MORTAL, APPEARS!

BUT NOW, THE BLOCK OF STONE THAT HAD HUNG BY A THREAD ABOVE SHAZAM'S THRONE CRASHES DOWN UPON THE WISE WIZARD!

SNAP!

SO IT IS WRITTEN, THAT I MUST GO!

CRASH!

BUT A MOMENT LATER, THE SPIRIT OF OLD SHAZAM ARISES AND GIVES CAPTAIN MARVEL INSTRUCTIONS!

I NAME YOU --- CAPTAIN MARVEL! THROUGH MY NAME YOU ARE GIVEN THE POWERS OF THESE SIX ELDER GODS! HENCEFORTH, YOU WILL FIGHT EVIL ON EARTH IN MY PLACE!

SOLOMON.. WISDOM
HERCULES.. STRENGTH
ATLAS.. STAMINA
ZEUS.. POWER
ACHILLES.. COURAGE
MERCURY.. SPEED

YES, SHAZAM!

AGAIN, MAGIC LIGHTNING THUNDERS DOWN, RETURNING CAPTAIN MARVEL TO THE FORM OF BILLY BATSON!

BOOM!

AND SECONDS LATER, BILLY FINDS HIMSELF AT HIS OLD POST!

GEE, IT ALL SEEMS LIKE A DREAM!

SUBWAY

72

True, one could suppose that the artist just had one standard face for mean old men, but that would be too simple. The more interesting supposition is that Dr. Sivana was Billy's uncle in disguise. Whether he wore a toupée, as the uncle did, or shaved off his hair, as Sivana did, is as unimportant as the other subtle changes in appearance. One can hardly believe that Sivana could fool Billy for long if he were not his uncle. Sivana and Billy were in fact members of the same family; good and evil sprang from the same blood.

Why else was Billy chosen from all the other honest and therefore poor newsboys in the world? Old Shazam was giving the boy a chance to help control the evilest man on Earth. Sivana was his cross to bear. If Billy never again recognized his uncle in his altered appearance as Sivana, chalk it up to a refusal to accept this terrible truth.

NOW, BACK TO OUR REGULAR PROGRAM.

The first of the many encounters between Captain Marvel and Dr. Sivana was over and, prophetically, it had ended in defeat for the self-proclaimed "Rightful Ruler of the Universe." As a reward for his part in the adventure, Sterling Morris, head of radio Station WHIZ, gave Billy a cushy job as a boy newscaster. Not only was he secretly the World's Mightiest Mortal, Billy had crashed into show biz. Things were surely going his way that weekend.

Billy Batson was going to run into a lot of trouble from a bunch of pushy characters—Ibac, gifted with the powers of four ancient villains, Captain Nazi, Mr. Banjo, and Mr. Mind, "the World's Wickedest Worm," and many others, as well as Sivana. But the job had its compensations. He got to travel a lot—to exotic places like Oklahoma City, Minneapolis, St. Louis. And in each of these cities Captain Marvel would solve some trifling problem like doing in a maniac who was trying to explode a dirigible full of laughing gas above City Hall so that the town could be looted while all the citizens laughed helplessly at the spectacle. The World's Mightiest Mortal would afterward accept the thanks of the mayor (unaccountably he had the face of Dizzy Dean— who broadcast the games of the local team—as if the artist had got the photographs he was to work from mixed up)

The chief artist for Captain Marvel, Clarence C. Beck, seldom made any mistakes, though his assistants slipped up from time to time. As he tells it himself (in a comic strip drawn for Jim Steranko's *History of Comics*), the head of Fawcett Publications sent for him in 1940 to create "the world's greatest cartoon character." Young C. C. Beck protested, "I'm an artist and illustrator—not a cartoonist!" The publisher, who strangely resembled Dr. Sivana, nodded. "I know, that's why I sent for you. All the cartoonists in town are busy—getting rich. . . . I'll pay you thirty dollars a week!"

The writer who worked with Beck on the concept of Captain Marvel was Bill Parker. Over the years, many others would contribute to the Marvel saga—editors Ed Herron and Wendell Crowley, artists Pete Costanza and (for one important issue, *Captain Marvel Adventures* No. 1) Jack Kirby. But no one contributed more than Otto Binder. A former science fiction writer (creator of the famous Adam Link, Robot short stories), Binder began work for Fawcett in 1941 and soon began scripting stories for Captain Marvel and the rest of the Marvel clan. By 1953 he had written 986 stories out of an approximate total of 1,743 for the whole series. It took the World's Mightiest Writer to keep up with the World's Mightiest Mortal. O. O. Binder and C. C. Beck were a Double-A team.

Of course, Beck did more than just draw. Captain Marvel reflected Beck's own personality. He changed lines of dialogue here and there, put in some "little" detail (when the captain knocked Sivana upside down, the little fiend cried „¡dʃəH„ upside down). Binder was Captain Marvel's brains, supplying his plots, but Beck was Marvel's funnybone. Behind his white beard, the old wizard Shazam was really C. C. Beck, dishing out magic from nine to five.

Captain Marvel was so popular that he was soon launched into his own magazine. (To make things rough on collectors, there are *four* important first issues for the World's Mightiest Mortal: *Whiz Comics, Special Edition Comics, Captain Marvel Thrill Book,* and *Captain Marvel Adventures.*) Even tougher to find than the Captain Marvel first issues —impossible, in fact—is the first, and only, issue of *Thunder Comics* in which Captain Marvel was called "Captain Thunder." It existed only in proof sheets inside the publisher's office. No issues were ever sold. The name "Captain Thunder" was changed to Captain Marvel right on the metal engravings. Everything else remained the same. But the printer got confused and numbered the first issue of *Whiz* as No. 2. (A number of first issues of comic books are confusingly labeled No. 2 because an issue that existed in proof sheets only was sent direct to the copyright office, before the first newsstand sale, as double protection against grabby, imitative competitors. But first-hand witnesses relate that *Thunder Comics* was not even copyrighted before the fateful change to *Whiz Comics* featuring Captain Marvel.)

Later years would bring the good Captain a sort of adopted son—Captain Marvel, Junior—and a sister, Mary Marvel, as well as other Marvels who appeared occasionally. Fawcett was making nothing but money.

Captain Marvel was appearing in his own magazine; in *The Marvel Family* along with Captain Marvel, Jr. and Mary Marvel; in *Whiz Comics* with Spy Smasher, Ibis the magician, and cowboy archer Golden Arrow; in *America's Greatest Comics* with Bulletman, Minute Man, and Mr. Scarlet. There were also miniature Captain Marvel comics, about 4 x 5 inches, and toys, games, sweatshirts, and so forth. The Captain Marvel Club grew by the millions, offering colorful pin-backs of several different designs and a club card with the World's Mightiest Code. (Perhaps at this late date it can be revealed that the code was simply the alphabet backwards— Z for A, Y for B, and so on.) One of the best things about being in the club was that Captain Marvel sent you a personal letter each month urging you to Collect Scrap to Beat a Jap and advising you of some of the outstanding stories coming up in Fawcett comic magazines.

They were outstanding enough to even outsell Superman.

The publishers of Superman did not like another super-powered being taking most of their action. A lawsuit was instigated that ran on for a decade. Fawcett finally threw in the cape when the sales of all comic books had fallen drastically in the early fifties. The Fawcett staff then scattered to the winds. Beck himself went to Florida and opened an advertising agency.

Then in 1972, apparently after years of negotiations, the publishers of *Superman* bought all rights to *Captain Marvel* and began publishing their old competitor. If they wanted to imitate or satirize their own property (Superman) there was no law against that. Editorials cheerfully urged readers to buy their favorite, whether Superman or Captain Marvel; they had nothing to lose in this circulation war.

But the original Captain Marvel had been dormant for so long that another company had begun issuing comics about another character called Captain Marvel. So that now, although our hero is still called Captain Marvel in the body of the stories, the magazine and the feature strip inside it are called *Shazam* after the magic word he uses.

And drawing Captain Marvel again after nearly twenty years is Clarence C. Beck, as untouched by time as Billy Batson. More than a commercial success—and it is a success again, selling out half a million copies of the first revival issue—the return of Captain Marvel is the triumph of a work of popular art, too good to remain buried forever by legal squabbles, a strip as great as the legendary newspaper strips like *Buck Rogers, Dick Tracy, Pogo* and *Peanuts.* It is also the triumph of C. C. Beck, the illustrator who created the world's mightiest cartoon character.

NO. 4

MARCH–APRIL

ALL STAR Comics

10¢

JUSTICE SOCIETY OF AMERICA

FOR AMERICA AND DEMOCRACY

Featuring

THE FLASH – THE SPECTRE – DR. FATE –
THE GREEN LANTERN – THE HAWKMAN –
THE HOUR-MAN – THE SANDMAN –
THE ATOM, AND JOHNNY THUNDER
*in the first complete book-length adven-
ture of the Justice Society of America*

REST OF THE SUPER FLOCK

There were dozens of other publishers bringing out hundreds of comic magazines a month during the "Golden Age" of comics in the forties. Some, like Dell, stuck mainly to reprinting newspaper comics such as *Flash Gordon* and *Little Orphan Annie.* However, most of them had their own superhero stars; the Human Torch and the Sub-Mariner (fire and water personified) and Captain America (Jack Kirby lending his own genius to a kind of patriotic Batman) starred at the Marvel group. The MLJ line had its Shield (a patriotic Superman), Steel Sterling (a rival also claiming to be "the Man of Steel") and the Black Hood. The Quality Comics Group had exquisitely beautiful artwork, by all-time super-genius Will Eisner on *The Spirit* and *Uncle Sam,* by Jack Cole on *Plastic Man,* by Lou Fine on *Black Condor,* and by Reed Crandall on *Blackhawk* and *The Ray* (and, except in Eisner's and Cole's cases, boring, routine stories). Behind all these artists and all these starring characters were a host of lesser talents and lesser characters. In many ways it resembled the old studio system—MGM (Superman DC Publications), Warner Bros. (Captain Marvel's Fawcett), 20th Century-Fox (glossy but slightly shallow Quality) and Monogram (Centaur Publications with Amazing Man, the Shark, the Iron Skull).

Yet in some way or another all these hundreds of magazines with thousands of heroes were only variations on Superman and Batman and the mightiest of mortals, Captain Marvel.

SOME SERIOUS PRICES FOR FUNNY BOOKS

These magazines have been known to sell for $1,000 or more in excellent condition:
Action Comics No. 1 (introducing Superman); June, 1938
Superman No. 1; Summer, 1939
These magazines have been known to sell for $500 or more in excellent condition:
Detective Comics No. 27 (introducing Batman); May, 1939
Batman No. 1; Spring, 1940
Marvel Mystery Comics No. 1; November, 1939
Whiz Comics No. 1 but marked "No. 2" (introducing Captain Marvel); February, 1940
These magazines have been known to sell for $200 or more in excellent condition:
Special Edition Comics No. 1 (first all-Captain Marvel issue); 1940
Captain America No. 1; March, 1941
Famous Funnies No. 1; 1934
Walt Disney's Comics and Stories No. 1; October 1940
These magazines have been known to sell for $150 or more in excellent condition:
All-Star Comics No. 1, No. 2, No. 3, No. 4; 1940
Human Torch No. 1 but marked "No. 2"; 1940
Captain Marvel Adventures No. 1 (first of regular series); 1941
Flash Comics No. 1; 1940
Flash Gordon, Dell Four Color No. 10 (the first Flash Gordon number in this variety series)
King Comics No. 1; 1936
Tarzan Single Series No. 20
Prince Valiant Feature Book 26
More Fun Comics No. 52, No. 53 (The Spectre begins)

NO. 4
ALL
SPRING ISSUE
WINNERS
10¢
WAR
A AVISON
CAPTAIN AMERICA HUMAN TORCH SUB MARINER DESTROYER WHIZZER
BATTLE FOR VICTORY FOR AMERICA

First issues of these magazines are now selling for $100 in excellent condition:

Ace Comics
Adventure Comics
All American Comics
All-Flash Quarterly
All-Winners
America's Greatest Comics
Big All-American (only issue)
Big Shot
Buck Rogers (Famous Funnies series)
Captain Marvel, Junior
Crack Comics
Daredevil Battles Hitler
Detective Comics
Green Lantern
Jumbo Comics
Jungle Comics
Leading Comics
More Fun Comics
Mystic Comics
Pep Comics
Planet Comics
Police Comics
Popular Comics
Sensation Comics
Shadow Comics
Shield-Wizard
Star-Spangled Comics
Sparkler Comics
Target Comics
Tom Mix Comics (Ralston giveaway)
Top Notch Comics
New York World's Fair Comics (1939 and 1940 editions)
World's Best Comics (later *World's Finest*)

The No. 2 issues of these titles are usually worth about 40% of the value of the first issue. The price structure then typically descends through the first ten issues by degrees to the point where issue No. 10 is often worth 20% of the value of the first issue. After the tenth issue, prices depend on the age of the comic or its special features.

Special Issues, particularly those containing the first appearances of famous characters, can be worth more than the first issue of the same magazine. The more celebrated "origin" issues have already been cited.

E. C. Comics began about 1950 and are the most valuable comics from that decade. *Tales from the Crypt, Weird Science, Weird Fantasy, Vault of Horror, Haunt of Fear, Crime SuspenStories* and any other comic from this period bearing the E.C. trademark in the corner is valuable—some are worth $15 or more in excellent condition. *Mad* No. 1 is worth about $60 and is edging up towards $100. A recent series of exact reprints of E.C. titles has been started. They are recognizable by the $1.00 cover price and the 1973 date inside. So far these are worth only the cover price.

Marvel Comics Group. Beginning with *Fantastic Four* No. 1 (November 1961), this group, under the editorship of Stan Lee (now Roy Thomas), has been the most popular with young people. *Fantastic Four* included a remodeled Human Torch, and other titles have brought back Captain America and the Sub-Mariner from the forties. Many new characters have been added, notably the troubled, even neurotic teen-aged *Spiderman.* All the early issues of these titles are reasonably valuable—*Fantastic Four* No. 1 is worth $60, and many later numbers are worth from $5 to $10. Many Marvel titles from the sixties are already worth $2 to $3. Marvel titles are the most valuable comics of the sixties.

The most valuable comics of the seventies may be the early revival issues of *Shazam* starring the original Captain Marvel. However, with some dealers stocking thousands of copies of the 1972 first issue of *Shazam,* it is hard to imagine that it will ever really be scarce.

Valuable Comics. Almost all old comics featuring fantastic and/or costumed characters, in fair to excellent condition, published between 1934 through 1942, are *very valuable* (worth anything from $15 to $1,000). These titles up to 1949 are *reasonably valuable* ($5 to $10). These titles after 1950 are of *some value* ($3 on down). After 1950, only E.C. titles and some special-interest issues (such as those with the art of Frazetta) are worth more than $10, generally speaking.

Worthless Comics. Any comic, regardless of age, with many defects (such as being coverless and also having pages out) is virtually worthless—although somebody may try to sell it for something, of course. Most funny animal comics *not* associated with Walt Disney or the Warners-Bugs Bunny group are virtually worthless, although an arbitrary price of 25¢ to $1.50 might be placed on them. Most romance, sports, and true story comics are similarly of little value, unless they are of very, very early vintage.

In conclusion, I can only say that comic collecting requires at least as much knowledge as stamp collecting. For those who are interested, a generally reliable and accurate 300-page guide to comic book values is available. It is *The Comic Book Price Guide* and it can be obtained from Robert Overstreet, Editor-Publisher, 2905 Vista Dr., N.W., Cleveland, Tennessee 37311. The price is $6 per copy.

They were real books, those Big Little Books, many with more than four hundred pages. Half of those pages were the text of the story, the other half the pictures—perhaps the most interesting part. Although kids called comics "comic books," they weren't really *books*—not like these, anyway.

I liked Big Little Books better than most comics. Although they were already going out of fashion by the time I was old enough to read them, I searched out copies from relatives and friends. New titles were still appearing, but the dime stores of my small home town didn't sell them. When I visited some thriving metropolis like Evansville, Indiana, I could pick up some of the later titles like *Roy Rogers* and *Bugs Bunny.* But the older ones were better—*Buck Jones, Flash Gordon, Mickey Mouse.*

Most of the BLBs were "novelized" from the comic strips and represented the first successful commercial reprinting from the comics. The first one of all, near the beginning of the thirties, was *Dick Tracy.* Some purists, such as Bill Blackbeard of the San Francisco Academy of Comic Art, condemn (more in sorrow than in anger) the BLBs for merely cannibalizing the strips, crudely doctoring out their dialogue balloons and substituting possibly unnecessary text to explain the panels.

The complaint has some merit, but the Big Little Books brought such joy to so many millions that it is hard to assess them severely. (The same Mr. Blackbeard tells how his Depression-stricken parents were once able to give him only one present at Christmastime during the thirties— a copy of *Mickey Mouse at Blaggart Castle*—and recalls that he did not feel particularly short-changed.)

The books were as permanent and solid as they looked. They survived the eager hands of childhood better than comics, and were kept more often, so that they are now generally less rare and less expensive. They average about three dollars each. The most expensive Big Little Book—a Cocomalt giveaway edition of *Buck Rogers in the City of Floating Globes*—costs only about thirty-five dollars.

It is not uncommon to find Big Little Books mixed in with "real" books among private collections purchased by book stores. *Flash Gordon and the Water World of Mongo* nestles beside *Pilgrim's Progress. Dick Tracy Out West* rubs shoulders with *The Gracie Allen Murder Case.* They were still valued as books by their former owners. Big Little Books may not have been great art—but, then again, they may have been. The serious interest in Alex Raymond's art for *Flash Gordon* continues to grow. Among those doing original illustrations for the BLBs was Henry Vallely, whose fine line work was of an austere purity that could almost be considered classical, as can be seen in *Jack Armstrong and the Ivory Treasure* or *Tom Mix and the Horde of Montezuma.*

Many of them had cracking good stories too. Maxwell Grant (privately, Walter Gibson) wrote a special BLB about his most famous character, *The Shadow and the Living Dead.* The verbal descriptions of some of those scenes remained with me for years. The Shadow, cloak flaring, eyes burning beneath the brim of his slouch hat, blazing away at a veritable army of homicidal zombies coming up the stairs to get him, coming, coming . . . more shots, then—no more ammunition! There was no way out. The Shadow would soon join these creatures in a state of living death. But from the darkness were thrust twin automatics, forty-fives, fully loaded, more welcome than water on the Sahara. The Shadow's faithful, mysterious "agents" had arrived. Those were the days!

Most of the Big Little Books were not quite so memorable. Many of them—perhaps most of them—were written by the late R. R. Winterbotham. I met Russ Winterbotham several times at science fiction conventions—a tall, leathery man with a mustache and thick, dark hair. Whenever we shared a drink together, I always got a secret thrill out of knowing that this was the man who had contributed so much to my childhood with such BLBs as *Captain Midnight and the Secret Squadron,* a marvelous original story, not just a comic strip rewrite. Winterbotham was never very informative

on how he wrote the Big Little Books, how he tried to keep the text in step with the illustration across from it (which did not always happen). He just "knocked them out," that was all. They'd say the same of Balzac.

There are some lucky souls who own a complete set of Whitman Publishing's Big Little Books. There are only about four hundred or so of them. Of course, there were the imitations of the Whitman volumes by other publishers—the Little Big Books from Saalfield, the Fast Action Books from Dell, Dime Action Books from Fawcett (four of them, to be exact: *Captain Marvel, Spy Smasher, Bulletman,* and *Minute Man),* Five Star Library, and others. Like real literature, the BLBs did not come out every month as the comic magazines did. There are only an even dozen *Flash Gordon* books from Whitman. Only two *Jungle Jims* in the regular line. Only one *Lightning Jim, U.S. Marshal.* Some people look for titles that never existed. There was never a *Prince Valiant* BLB, or one of *Superman,* although Whitman, like so many other publishers, offered its own competitor, *Maximo, the Amazing Superman.* There were movie adaptations, with still photographs reproduced, including *The Count of Monte Cristo* and *The Three Musketeers,* but never anything possibly "objectionable" like *Frankenstein* or *Dracula.*

It was the book format, with pages of text, that gave Big Little Books their true respectability. Aunts and uncles could give them as presents, although they might abhor the brightly colored comics. In fact, it was their respectability and aura of permanent value which contributed to their survival during the desperate thirties. In the more frantic forties, they lost out to the gaudier comic magazines. A few new titles came out, and there were several variations of format. Whitman even tried a new line of Big Little Books with full-color illustrations in the late sixties. They didn't succeed, for the BLBs belonged to the thirties—a time when even little pleasures were a big thing.

PULP MAGAZINES

BLACK CLOAKS & PURPLE PROSE

The last few pulp-paper magazines were tossed on the newsstands when I was a boy. The edges were ragged and untrimmed (it made them significantly cheaper to print) and the covers a lurid panorama of sex and violence. The paper inside was rough-textured—cheap pulp grade—and filled with text set in fairly large type, interrupted by black-and-white line drawings possessed of a raw vitality.

The subject matter was anything that suggested wild adventure, whether it took place in the jungles of Brazil, the moons of Saturn, the battle skies of World War I, or the gangster-infested streets of New York. Each subdivision had its own peculiar attributes, style, and favorite characters and plots.

Books and magazine articles refer to these magazines as "pulps" today, but originally that was a trade term, used only by writers and publishers. The average person called them by a lot of other names—fiction magazines, story magazines, thrillers, even "dime novels," although that term properly belongs to the Nick Carter and Buffalo Bill paperbacks from the turn of the century.

The pulps hit their heyday in the thirties. They were still around in the forties when I was old enough to read them, and they had changed relatively little. Even very late examples from 1956 of some struggling survivor like *Startling Detective* looked as if it might have been printed in 1935. Maybe that was their trouble. They couldn't change with the times and still remain what they were.

Pulps were the first "books" I read after Big Little Books. The first short stories I ever read were by Robert Bloch and Ray Bradbury in the pages of *Weird Tales.* Among the first novels I read were those by Henry Kuttner in *Startling Stories* and by Maxwell Grant in *The Shadow* Magazine. These stories were fun. They were exciting and, to a small boy, enlightening and meaningful. Some of them still are to a grown man. I learned a love of reading and writing from the pulps. I became a reader, a fan, a collector, a writer. They helped shape my life.

I suppose I might have grown up to be a vampire or an astronaut—certainly some pulp readers have done one or the other—but I became one who wrote about such things instead. By the time I was old enough to write for the pulps when I was in my teens, there was only one line of magazines left in the old original pulp format, the Double-Action Group. During their last year of existence I turned out stories for *Real Western, Famous Detective, Science Fiction Quarterly,* and others. Fortunately, I outlived the source of my inspiration.

But more than professionally, the pulps gave me an affinity for things beyond the commonplace —the absurd, the grotesque, the nonconformist. I've learned to selectively reject what others value, and sometimes to value what others reject. The pulps themselves are one of these things.

Damned by critics and educators as corrupting trash designed to turn all their readers into mindless, shambling sex fiends and ax murderers, the pulps nevertheless produced a group of significant writers like Ray Bradbury, Dashiel Hammett, Evan Hunter, and Kurt Vonnegut, Jr.

But it is almost unimportant that some pulp stories could aspire to greatness—they were more than great; they were *terrific!*

The best of pulp stories are told at a level of *intensity* felt by both the writer and the reader. People, places and events loom larger than life. Their descriptions may seem lurid or overblown to the uninvolved. But in real life, many things may take on greater dimensions, as when a man is in love on the one hand or fighting for his life on the other. (Or, in some cases, finding himself involved in both situations at the same time.)

I am not sure who first distilled the idea, but it has been observed on numerous occasions that the pulp story is dedicated to the principle that a man never lives life so fully as when he is in immediate danger of losing it. Pulp heroes (and, vicariously at least, pulp readers) were like today's mountain-climbers and sky-divers—they enjoyed the heady thrill of danger as no other.

DOC SAVAGE

A STREET & SMITH PUBLICATION

SUMMER 1949
25 CENTS

UP FROM EARTH'S CENTER

By KENNETH ROBESON
A COMPLETE "DOC SAVAGE" NOVEL

DOC SAVAGE

Once upon a time, a boy named Clark Savage, Jr., was born and immediately put into the care of scientists and other experts to train him for his mission in life. The mission which his adventurer-father saw for him: "to go here and there, to the ends of the earth, if necessary, striving to help those in need of help, and punishing those who justly deserve it."

Strangely enough, the youngster did not rebel against all this force-feeding and turn ax-murderer. The good stock he came from—his mother must have been quite a woman herself—enabled him to survive even this horror of a childhood with his sanity intact. He became, in the words of one awe-struck character in the novels, "a specialist in electricity, chemistry, geology, engineering—and everything else! A specialist, mind you! Not a dabbler! They say none of the big shots in those lines are superior to Savage in learning. He can tell 'em all things about their own rackets."

Doc Savage—he obviously had Ph.D. degrees in enough sciences, including medicine, to claim the title—had not neglected physical education in his training course. He stood well over six feet, with bronzed muscle and fingers "as strong as most men's wrists." Nor did he let himself go to pot any time during his hectic sixteen-year career. The less modest supermen who advertised—Charles Atlas, Joe Bonomo, *et al.*—promised to make you, the reader, superhuman in only ten or fifteen minutes a day. Doc himself offered a similar course of exercises in the back pages of the magazine, but he didn't fool around himself with only a few minutes of daily training. He spent *two hours a day* at it.

The Savage program employed "since his cradle days . . . accounted for his terrific strength and the keenness of his senses. He made his muscles tug and strain against each other; he juggled complex mathematical problems in his head to sharpen his concentration. He had an apparatus which made sound waves of remote frequencies; he had an assortment of scores of different odors which he identified swiftly. A page or two of Braille printing developed his touch. He had many other things in his routine. Two hours of terrific work!"

Obviously, Doc Savage needed no one to help him do anything. Perhaps this was why he never had a girl. One could dismiss this as a matter of personal inclination, but it could not have been through incompetence, certainly. Though conceivably inexperienced in a few areas, Doc Savage could never be anything but expert at whatever he undertook. Even his five friends—his five aides—were not *needed*. Doc Savage probably was above such a mortal need as companionship, and although each was a genius in some branch of learning, Doc could, after all, tell *all* specialists "things about their own rackets." No, his letting these five characters tag him around was only another act of the boundless human kindness of which Doc was capable.

Leaders of commerce and industry, distinguished military officers though they were, this little group of experts acted just like a bunch of kids most of the time.

Colonel John Renwick—"Renny"—was a top engineer as well as an ex-army officer, but he had a passion for smashing his massive fists through the panels of locked doors. William Harper Littlejohn —"Johnny"—was the world's greatest living expert on archaeology and geology, but he gloried in an adolescent mania for an affected multisyllabic vocabulary, including such phrases as "I'll be superamalgamated." Major Thomas J. Roberts— "Long Tom"—was apparently a bit of a weakling who looked as if he were ready to fall into a swoon with a slight touch of plague, but he was an electrical genius second only to Edison. And then there were Doc's two major assistants, the only two who appeared in many of the later, somewhat shorter stories. Brigadier General Theodore Marley Brooks—"Ham"—was one of the nation's leading attorneys, and it was natural that he should be very concerned with his "sartorial splendor," but did his walking outfit *have* to include a sword cane? Finally, there was Lieutenant Colonel Andrew Blodgett Mayfair—"Monk"—who was only five feet tall but weighed over 260 pounds and had arms six inches longer than his legs. Monk was a master of chemistry. I suspect he got that way looking for a formula to turn himself back into Dr. Jekyll. He and Ham had a running feud over helping Doc and aiding girls in distress, but mostly over each other's appearances—the dude vs. the hairy ape.

When one *really* thinks about that crew, one must thank God for Doc Savage himself, who was called upon so often to save the world. Those five assistants, if left to themselves, might well have decided to run off and go on a panty raid while the world took care of itself.

Young Doc was stuck with his "Fabulous Five" right from the first issue of the *Doc Savage* Magazine in March, 1933. The story was called, reasonably enough, *The Man of Bronze.* When it came to metals, his greatest concern in this "origin" story was for the fabulous gold cache in the Central American country of Hidalgo (don't bother to check your atlas). His father's instructions, left in a posthumous message, led Doc to the prehistoric valley peopled by the lost civilization of Mayan Indians, where the gold lay. In his big-city office, Doc spoke to his crew of the adventure they were about to begin, which would lead to so many more adventures.

"We first got together back in the War," he told the five slowly. "We all liked the big scrap. It got into our blood. When we came back, the humdrum life of an ordinary man was not suited to our natures. So we sought something else."

Doc held their absolute attention, as if he had them hypnotized. Undeniably this golden-eyed man was the leader of the group, as well as leader of anything he undertook. His very being denoted a calm knowledge of all things, and an ability to handle himself under any conditions.

"Moved by mutual admiration for my father," Doc continued, "we decided to take up his work of good wherever he was forced to leave off . . . We at once began training ourselves for that purpose. It is the cause for which I had been reared from the cradle, but you fellows, because of a love of excitement and adventure, wish

to join me . . . Tonight . . . we begin carrying out the ideals of my father . . ."

The gold they liberated from Hidalgo enabled Doc and his friends to carry on their good works, beginning in *The Man of Bronze* and continuing on through scores of later exploits. Their adventures took them to other prehistoric climes in *The Land of Terror,* to New York City in 1939 to meet *The World's Fair Goblin,* to the American West to plumb the dangers of *The Derrick Devil,* to the fringes of the unknown to combat *The Mental Monster,* and finally, in the summer of 1949, to his final adventure, *Up from Earth's Center.* What came "up" were the inhabitants of Hell itself. Oh, there was a bit of hedging—it might have been a hoax or hallucination—but we knew that, like Orpheus, Doc Savage could visit the Land of the Dead and return alive.

In his final exploit, Doc Savage wrestled Satan himself and won! What else? Yet even Doc, as he fought the minions of Hell, for the first time knew naked fear.

Suddenly, Doc screamed, probably the first shriek of unadulterated terror he had given in his lifetime. He kicked wildly at the creature, which had buried its bony claws in his legs . . . The tentacles of the creature that embraced him, indeed the thing's whole body, felt spongy and slimy, and about it was the odor Monk had noted, the sickening odor of fear . . . He remembered then about their fear of flame . . . He fumbled insanely in his pockets, found his cigarette lighter and thumbed it into flame. Instantly, the repulsive thing flew away from him, covering many feet in one leap, and flattened itself against the broken stone, wailing with maniacal terror. Doc Savage sprang to his feet, more filled with fear than he had ever been, and began running . . .

Such an experience might well make any man decide it was time to retire and enjoy life for a time. Although by harsh chronological calculations, Doc must be in his sixties today, I can't imagine him sitting around quietly forever. He will probably be the first senior citizen astronaut.

Unfortunately, there will never be any further *real* Doc Savage novels to relate his adventures. The author of most and all of the best of the Savage stories, the man behind the pen name "Kenneth Robeson," Lester Dent, is dead. He was a prolific writer and a striking stylist. His work seems crude at first glance, but reveals a studied simplicity on closer examination. He was an idea man, too. He could get the nuttiest ideas for stories, and then carry them off in a way many others couldn't. He was also noted for his remarkable openings, his "narrative hooks." For example, the 1943 novel, *Hell Below,* began: "'I used to fight Indians,' the old gentleman said. 'I used to eat their ears. I would stew their ears, then eat them with salt.'"

Lester Dent never got himself confused with his creation. He never thought he was doing anything but writing *about* a remarkable man. Through the actions of Doc Savage, author Dent naturally revealed many of his own views about life—but not about love. Never, never was there anything vaguely resembling a love scene between Doc and any girl. Despite that, there can never be any serious doubt as to the virility of Doc or, by inference, of his creator.

In later years, Dent went on to write more "serious" adult works, including ones about a tycoon-detective named "Chance" Malloy. Perhaps Malloy was not precisely Doc Savage under another name, but his attitude—Lester Dent's own attitude—toward the fairer sex was one that Doc himself would not have found foreign to his ideals. Dent's later hero saw a woman not as a moment of sensual pleasure, but as a whole human being capable of giving and deserving love, as shown by his line of thought in *Lady to Kill* (Doubleday, 1946).

He carried many pleasant memories of a
skiing trip in Idaho, a week in Mexico; one of
his nicest recollections was of a sparkling
Martha on wild-flying skis against a majestic
backdrop of mountains and diamond-dust
snow, trimming him in a downhill slalom,
and it was perfectly natural he should recall
something like that more clearly than being
in bed with Martha.

Such mysteries gave Dent a wider latitude of
adult emotions to employ, but the ephemera of pulp
writing was what endured.

Remembered and collected for years by a hard
core of fans, the Doc Savage novels were finally
reprinted by Bantam Books in paperback. But those
neat rectangles on the paperback racks cannot catch
all the charm of the dog-eared pulps with their
outrageous cover scenes, their fascinating,
compelling blurbs. The soft-cover editions have
added only one feature, and that one is decidedly
not an improvement. Doc has been adorned with
a repulsive crewcut whose widow's peak reaches to
the bridge of his nose. This attempt to make him
resemble a sadistic former Nazi SS man was
apparently designed to appeal to all the Mike
Hammer fans in the audience with a passion for
cruel-eyed brutes. (The artwork by Bama *is*
striking, however.)

"The Code of Doc Savage," which always
appeared somewhere in the pulp magazine, has
been neglected by the paperback publishers. But
then no hard-eyed killer ever followed this "Code."
Perhaps no one but Doc Savage ever *could*
completely live up to it.

Let me strive, every moment of my life,
to make myself better and better, to the
best of my ability, that all men may profit
by it. Let me think of the right, and lend all
my assistance to those who need it, with no
regard for anything but Justice. Let me take
what comes with a smile, without loss of
courage. Let me be considerate of my country,
of my fellow citizens and my associates in
everything I say and do. Let me do right to
all, and wrong to no man.

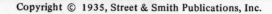

A STREET & SMITH PUBLICATION

THE
Shadow
MAGAZINE
TWICE A MONTH

10 CENTS

LINGO
80 Page
Detective
Novel

94

THE SHADOW

Sliding through the gloom of night, virtually invisible beneath the sweep of his black cape, his hawklike features shaded into obscurity by the brim of his slouch hat, The Shadow stalked his prey. In either hand was a heavy .45 automatic. First one patch of darkness, then another, concealed the Master of Darkness. Behind him, he felt his trademark on the night wind—a whispered chill of mocking laughter.

The haunting laugh of The Shadow was shattered by gunfire. From an alleyway poured a horde of criminals. The Shadow knew them. The rats of the underworld—narrow, cunning faces beneath billed caps, broader, more brutal countenances under grease-stained derbies. He knew them all. He had met them in a thousand encounters. They had names like "Konk Zitz," "Crowdy Sokolos," "Shag Korman," and that slimiest of weasels, "Moocher Gleetz." The Shadow opened fire!

His twin automatics poured forth a steady stream of burning steel at the herd of crooks. The Shadow's bullets "cowed them" and "sent them staggering"; the "slugs whistling about their ears" "withered them." As The Shadow's triumphant laugh rolled out, it was answered by "cries of pain. . . whimpers. . . curses. . . gasps. . ."

The "taunting" fire of The Shadow was overwhelming to the cringing hoodlums. They "screeched" in stumbling panic in response to his "big guns," those "heavy automatics," the "mammoth .45s." They had never seen the like. Ineffectively, they plinked away at the confusing shifting of shadows with their comparatively toy-like .32s and .38s. The answering scorn of The Shadow's laugh for these effete splats of lead brought forth "sobs of despair" from the gangland delegation.

It happened like that a thousand times. One specific case occurred in *The Red Blot* by Maxwell Grant, *The Shadow* Magazine, June 1, 1933.

A squad of mobsmen were tumbling into the space beside the bank, opening fire upon this unexpected enemy who had entered the path which they had left open for retreat. . . Well had The Shadow planned! He had waited until the crooks had broken through, and had started the alarms. Now, by swift attack, he was harassing them while the law was on the way. . . Blasts from the automatics came at regular intervals. When mobsters fired, The Shadow was no longer there. The strange battle continued; then came the clang of a police car, swinging from the distance. . .

Policemen, entering the space by the front of the bank building, stopped as they heard a cry which reverberated through the narrow passage. The tones of a triumphant, mocking laugh—a weird burst of mirth that seemed to come from another sphere!

The laugh of The Shadow.

We read it all and accepted it without question then, but now questions do come to mind. The questions can't really harm so classic a figure of fantasy as The Shadow; they can only reveal the tantalizing paradoxes of his character.

If The Shadow wished to conceal himself in the darkness, why was the lining of his great black cloak a bright scarlet? Why did he wear a flashing, fiery girasol ring on one hand? These two touches of red must have flashed from time to time, spotlighting him like a Christmas tree topped by a slouch hat. This was concealment, secrecy, furtiveness?

Those "big guns" of The Shadow, how the miserable little rats of the underworld envied them. *Nobody* else in the The Shadow's universe ever dared carry a similar weapon—no cop, no crook, not even a retired army officer who may have received one as standard issue. The criminal element constantly were awed by those "heavy automatics," those "mammoth .45s"; in short, those Colt Model 1911A1 firearms. But crooks were, after all, un-American quitters and failures who didn't know how to dream the big dream. None of them ever went out and knocked over a pawnshop to get a pair of .45s for himself.

But why did the crooks envy those guns of The Shadow so much? After all, he never hit anybody with them.

Remember, The Shadow's shots sent crooks "howling" and "cowering"; they brought forth "howls," "gasps," "curses." But those bullets seldom if ever actually *hit* or *killed* anybody. It was a matter of all these scurvy little hoods with their dinky little effeminate .38s being pestered by this tall guy in an opera cloak who was laughing this crazy laugh all the time and triggering away on two .45s for all he was worth, sending bullets "whistling," "singing," even "rasping" by, but never striking—*plop*. Every night of the week he was out, cutting away with those .45s. More than one of the crooks must have thought, "If he keeps this up long enough, somebody is going to get hurt!" It certainly wasn't The Shadow who was going to be hurt. The gangland punks were even poorer shots than he was. Their bullets didn't even annoy him as his did them.

The Shadow must have got off a few hundred rounds of ammunition in an average night's escapade. But a .45 automatic only holds eight shells, one in the chamber and seven in the clip. Eight shots are no more than necessary to send one little weasel "cowering" and "staggering." The sixteen shots from two automatics wouldn't last much longer—only seconds in fact. With a dozen gunmen blasting away at him—the din, if nothing else, must have been murder—The Shadow must have been kept busy just changing clips.

Despite it all, The Shadow returned to the fray again and again. Of the some ten to fifteen million words written about The Shadow under the byline of Maxwell Grant, fully one-third of the verbiage must have concerned such gun battles, although there was not one word, so far as I know, about the Master of Darkness reloading his weapons.

Taking up a somewhat smaller amount of space were the frequent scenes of Lamont Cranston's chats with his friend, Police Commissioner Ralph Weston, at the exclusive Cobalt Club. What a contrast between this world and that of dingy alleyways frequented by hoodlums! What person, besides everybody's mother and father, could possibly fear that reading pulp magazines might lead one into a life of crime? Who could want to be like one of those ratty little crooks, with their sweaters and billed caps, with their cigarette butts dangling from weak mouths? Even if you read the magazine by candlelight because the electricity

had been shut off, you knew you belonged to the atmosphere of the Cobalt Club, you belonged with the good guys. The good guys all wore felt hats of a certain latitude of style—snapbrim, fedora or, in one case, slouch—and they didn't have cigarette butts dangling from the corners of their mouths. Cranston and Weston sat around in big leather chairs and smoked "thin cigars." Never in my whole life, until I was twenty-five maybe, did I see a "thin" cigar—they were all fat and thick and usually sort of black. But somehow, without ever seeing one, you knew a "thin" cigar had to have *class.*

Who would want to be whimpering and scurrying about beneath the whistling shots of The Shadow when he could be with socialite Lamont Cranston and Commissioner Weston as they savored their narrow Havanas? Who would want to be called "Moocher" when he could be called "Lamont"?

During some nineteen years, Commissioner Weston (no mere cop but something of a social figure himself) never once suspected razor-nosed, stinking-rich Lamont Cranston of being anything but a sleepy-eyed cigar smoker. Blithely, Weston babbled all the secret plans of the N.Y.P.D. while Cranston blew rings around him. With the divine human kindness of which only superhuman heroes are capable, Cranston would drop a hint or offer a suggestion that would help the commissioner crack the case wide open. Then, excusing himself for a telephone call (never a call of nature), Cranston would slip into a deserted hallway and peel out a long, black cloak and a slouch hat from his briefcase and disappear into the night, trailing a peculiar laugh.

However, be it understood, The Shadow seldom went into action immediately. He required a period of contemplation, the third of the pivotal scenes of all the Shadow stories. The Shadow had to be himself at times. As faithful readers knew, he was not really Lamont Cranston, but only *posed* as him. According to the story *The Crime Ray*, published September 1, 1939, "There was a real Lamont Cranston—a big-game hunter and world traveler, and, known to him, while he was away The Shadow would adopt his identity." It was The Shadow's favorite pose—obviously, the appearance and personality must have been akin to The Shadow's own—but he had other guises he fabricated, including Lingo Queed, a slouchy minor minion of the underworld, and Henry Arnaud, a graying businessman. The Shadow had *once* been Kent Allard, a World War One aviator presumed dead, but that was not precisely his true identity. The Shadow had been The Shadow so long, *that* was who he *really* was, and no one else.

The Shadow could only be fully himself in his secret sanctum. As *The Red Blot* had it:

He, alone, visited this mystic room, located in some unknown section of Manhattan. In the midst of strenuous campaigns, The Shadow could always seek the seclusion of this sanctuary, there to mock his enemies and devise new ways to end the schemes of malefactors... Thus The Shadow found complete seclusion in that corner of the black-walled room where blue light shone upon a table top... Into the circle of illumination crept two objects that seemed like living creatures detached from the body to which they belonged.

The hands of The Shadow!

Long and white, they showed a combination of velvet smoothness and great muscular power... One of them bore the token which was the positive symbol of The Shadow.

This mark was a gleaming gem which shone from the third finger of the left hand. It was The Shadow's girasol, a rare fire opal, unmatched in all the world... From the girasol came splashes of fiery light, like the glimmer of living sparks. A dying ember, ever emitting its final darts of minute flame—such was The Shadow's girasol.

The hands moved in a fashion that portrayed ease of operation. An envelope came into view; from it a thin bundle of papers. The fingers unfolded a sheet; the hidden eyes behind the light made a brief perusal; then that paper was replaced by another. . .

For hours at a time, and for page after page in countless novels, The Shadow played around in his private sanctuary, admiring his pretty white hands and his nice shiny ring, and reading messages under his funny blue light, writing cryptic notes which he promptly destroyed, chuckling, laughing, wiggling his fingers, watching the girasol catch the light, opening a new envelope, and finally switching off the strange blue light and slipping away before dawn, before They could catch up with him. (The Shadow *knew* They were after him.)

Those messages in the envelopes did come from somewhere other than The Shadow's imagination. The Shadow did have a lot of agents out in the field to aid him in his war on crime. He had no faithful Indian companion, but he had a trusted Jewish aide, Moe Shrevnitz, a cabbie who was frequently alleged to be "crafty" with little apparent justification: Moe, or "Shrevie" as he was called, used to pick up Cranston or The Shadow and drive them anywhere and everywhere at any hour of the night or day, without ever getting paid, much less tipped.

Harry Vincent, handsome, competent, youthful, was the prime agent of The Shadow. In the very first story, *The Living Shadow* (Winter, 1931), the Master of Darkness saved Harry's life when he prevented him from swan-diving off a bridge. "Your life. . . belongs to me now. . . I shall improve it. . . life, with enjoyment, with danger, with excitement. Life, above all, with honor. And in return, I demand obedience." During the next two decades, on more than one occasion, Harry must have wished he had jumped.

There were other Shadow agents: "Hawkeye," small-time crook turned informer; Clyde Burke, star reporter for the New York *Classic,* who must have wondered how come he never managed to land his *own* series, like most other reporters; and of course Margo Lane, the "striking brunette" who was one of The Shadow's "loyal agents" if not as apparently his "friend and companion" in the pulp pages as she was on the radio series. She hadn't originally come from the pen of Maxwell Grant; she was only "feedback" from the radio program, and the writer seemed to employ her under protest.

There were scenes with incidental characters and scenes from the crooks' viewpoint. But the crooks were a pretty uninteresting lot, small-timers with plans for robbing banks or stealing rare paintings. The leaders sometimes gave themselves mildly colorful names like the Red Blot, the Harvester, or the Yellow Mask, but most of them didn't even bother. They realized how much they were overshadowed by The Shadow.

Most of the Shadow stories from 1931 to the last one, *The Whispering Eyes* in the spring of 1949, were written by Walter Gibson under the name of Maxwell Grant. Gibson had once been a professional magician, and his stories were based on the magician's trick of misdirection. Nothing much was really happening, but you were distracted from the fact by all the hangups and idiosyncrasies of The Shadow. It was one vast card trick, and Gibson kept playing the same cards over and over—gunfight, Cobalt Club, secret sanctum.

The Shadow was a perfect pulp character, because he was one that the relatively low-paid pulp writer like Gibson-Grant could go on writing words upon words about indefinitely, at a penny a word (or more later).

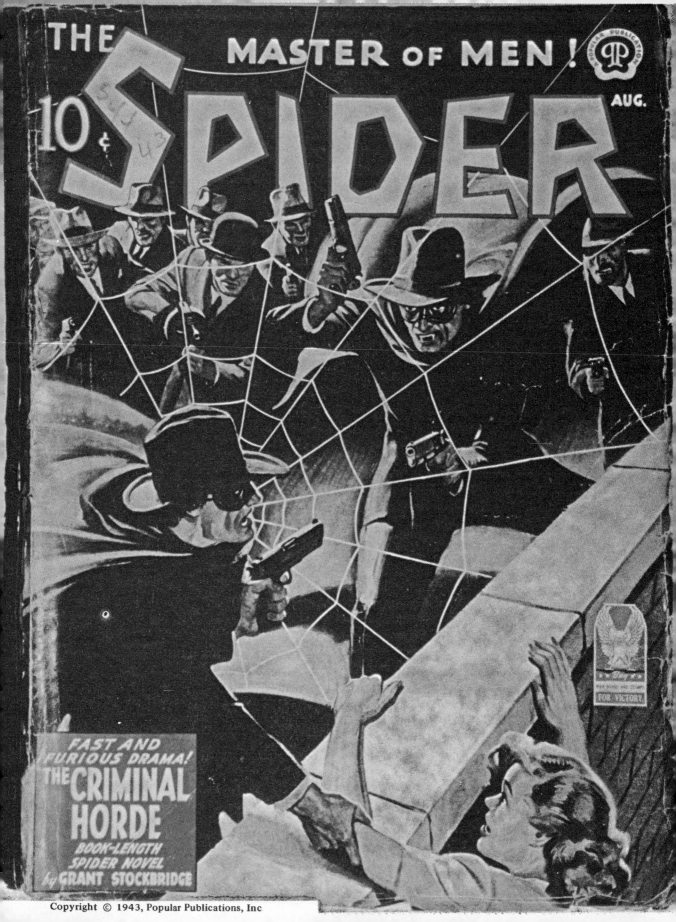

THE
MASTER of MEN!
10¢
SPIDER
AUG.

FAST AND FURIOUS DRAMA!
THE CRIMINAL HORDE
BOOK-LENGTH SPIDER NOVEL
by GRANT STOCKBRIDGE

THE SPIDER

One man always seemed to stand engulfed in the trailing cloak of The Shadow. No matter how different or unique he might be himself, he was forever compared to Street & Smith's earlier weirdly laughing avenger. The two men had their similarities: both wore cloaks, both fought crime, both seemed mad at times. But if the madness of The Shadow was harmless to those crooks always successfully scurrying away from his gun work, insanity ran far deeper and more dangerously in the case of his greatest rival, The Spider.

The first issue of *The Spider* Magazine appeared in October, 1933, two years after the first issue of *The Shadow*. A *Spider* radio show originating from KMOX, St. Louis, followed The Shadow's successful series on the air. There was a movie serial based on The Spider starring Warren Hull, but only after Rod LaRoque and Victor Jory had successfully portrayed The Shadow on the screen.

The true Spider could only be found in the pages of his own magazine, however. He couldn't pass media censorship anywhere else. Richard Wentworth, alias The Spider, was a practicing homicidal maniac, and that was only one aspect of his particular mental syndrome. The dimensions of his sickness remain awesome even today. Not only did Wentworth derive sexual and spiritual satisfaction from murder, he enjoyed a death wish of his own, he was tormented by a father fixation, and he was electrified by occasional flashes from his Messiah complex.

The Spider's atmosphere of death, fear, corruption, depravity, violence and sheer nuttiness must be experienced to be believed. Even on re-reading today the character and the stories retain a vital strain of raw interest. The writer "Grant Stockbridge" (really novelist and war correspondent Norvell Page) believed in The Spider and the web and woof of his world. He visualized the emotional reactions of Richard Wentworth and the substance of his surroundings with a vitality missing from the work of other pulpsters who wrote for money and perhaps a certain measure of craftsmanlike satisfaction. The Spider's chronicler, after all, wrote to express his own and his hero's unique philosophy of life.

That philosophy was reflected even in the style in which the stories were written. Both style and philosophy belonged to that universe of thought and feeling which is impossible to define adequately but which is always recognized on sight by those familiar with it as Pulp.

In the world of Pulp, a fat man lumbers across the pages with the awesome pachydermic mass of a grounded Moby Dick; a beautiful woman is lovely enough to entice a Father Brown away from his table, his bottle, and his vows; a villain is evil enough to make Fagin look like a good candidate for a male den mother. It was this Pulp World that led to the moral breakdown of Richard Wentworth. Most pulp heroes really had no personal philosophy at all, being merely as charmingly right-thinking as Barry Goldwater. Wentworth had a strong personal credo, but one that became fixedly wrong. Being a part of the very grain of Pulp, Wentworth carried things too far.

Perhaps if he had been a real person, not a fictional character, Wentworth could have been saved simply by having someone say to him: "Being against evil is quite all right, old man, but let's not get ridiculous about it, shall we?" Unfortunately nobody ever said it.

In order to murder in the name of justice, The Spider disguised himself for his midnight prowls about his city. He wore a black cloak and slouch hat, not unlike his colleague The Shadow, but he furthered his sinister image by altering his manly figure and clean-cut good looks to resemble a hook-nosed, fanged hunchback. (The hump served a useful purpose as well: when The Spider had to leave a skyscraper or a bridge abruptly, he could just jump off and float down on the parachute concealed in it.)

Occasionally, Wentworth would be too pressed for time to assume all the complex make-up it took to transform him into the hunchback. On these occasions, he used only the hat and cloak and a small, Lone Ranger-type domino mask, but being The Spider he added one distinction. The mask was not made of cloth. It was fashioned from *blued steel.*

Yet Wentworth's disguise as The Spider was not the man. His true identity remained Richard Wentworth. That is, in contrast to The Shadow's posing as Lamont Cranston but remaining really The Shadow, Richard Wentworth often went through most of a novel without ever assuming either the steel mask or hunchback make-up of The Spider, and there was so little difference between what he did as Wentworth and his behavior as The Spider that many of the cast of characters knew that they were one and the same, but only lacked solid "proof."

Although he was not averse to killing as Wentworth, The Spider had to employ his more spectacular disguise for his wilder rampages. In the course of an average novel, The Spider slaughtered between thirty and fifty human beings. Although at the end of *The Mayor of Hell* (1936) Wentworth stated, "I never have been able to kill a man in cold blood," he had been known to shoot alleged criminals through an open window as they were sitting at a table "planning crimes." In *Master of the Death-Madness* (1935), he considered going in and killing an elderly man in his sleep because he sensed "something evil" about him. The Spider was especially proficient in extracting information from a cringing crook under threat of death, but the "squealer" seldom did himself any good; The Spider found a reason to kill him anyway. "He was a rat," was often grounds enough.

The Spider's most typical homicides would occur in a blazing gunfight. Against overwhelming odds, he would blast down four to twelve men, killing them by shooting them through the head, heart or guts. He had the same superhuman skill with his guns, the same skill at dodging the bullets of others, as The Shadow. Presumably he could panic his foes with nonlethal "snarling bullets" in the manner of The Shadow, or even shoot their guns out of their hands like the Lone Ranger, or deliberately knock them out by "creasing their skulls" as Tom Mix used to do on the radio. But it was a conscious decision of The Spider to shoot to kill.

All of those heroic alternatives were unreal, though The Spider's own virtuoso skill at murder was no more "realistic." But perhaps death lends an artificial reality to this fantasy. Death can give a meaning to the shallowest of dramatics, but here it was a dark meaning indeed. The men The Spider shot were *dead*. It was not a question of James Thurber's scored-upon fencer picking up his head or of Roy Barcroft's returning time and again after falling under the guns of Gene Autry or Richard Boone. The victims of The Spider were DEAD.

Wentworth used both revolvers from the hip, shooting them independently. He did not have to aim. From the first day he had donned the mantle of The Spider, he had realized that his life would frequently depend upon the accuracy of his fire and he had practiced with an intensity few men could equal. He had duplicated every feat of gun-fire ever recorded.

Wentworth's two guns blasted together and two policemen went down, already dead with their bullet-pierced hearts. . .

The red-faced policeman was tottering on his feet, arms flung wide, gasping for air. Blood was beginning to stain the breast of his tunic. . . The cop's face was twisted, his eyes very wide, so that the white showed. His hat sat crazily on his head with the visor over one ear.

Wentworth saw all those things as he whipped over his thirty-eight and pulled the trigger. . . The man's face had vanished and in its place was a bloody smear . . .

As it turned out, the *coup de grace* for the florid-faced cop came from the gun of Stanley Kirkpatrick, one-time police commissioner.

Wentworth's heart lifted a little. If Kirkpatrick had done that, he must have known past any doubt that these cops were crooks. Otherwise, nothing could have driven him to the murderous attack . . .

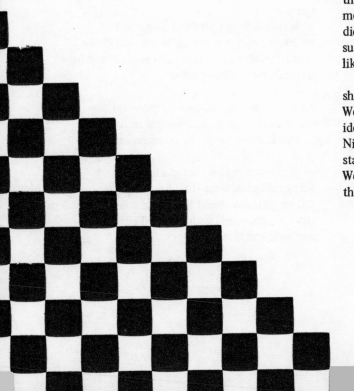

In this particular gun battle, one of twenty or so in *The Mayor of Hell,* The Spider killed five men himself; six others, friend and foe, were slaughtered. Kirkpatrick was severely wounded.

Unlike The Shadow, The Spider was frequently wounded, virtually shot to pieces, with bullets in the lungs, stomach, brain and other supposedly vital organs. Of course, for Wentworth this was just "heavy petting" with his love, Death. And Death could only consummate their love by taking him virgin, and only once.

The bite of bullets caressed The Spider time after time in *Master of the Death-Madness* until . . .

Wentworth's shoulder struck back hard against the glass barrier. He knew an instant of commingled pain, self-mockery and despair. For a long moment, he stood, spread-eagled against the bullet-proof panel. Deliberately, shouting incoherent words, the policeman fired again.

The Spider crumpled forward on his face . . .

Of course, Wentworth was not really dead. The Spider could not die, and of course never did really die in the whole course of the magazine's history. For purely commercial reasons, one does not kill the goose that lays several hundred thousand salable magazine copies every two months. More subjectively, The Spider could not die because that would mark the end of his suffering. He could only seem to die, to arise again like some mythical or religious figure.

Nina Talbot, Wentworth's erstwhile fiancee, shared his love of death. She shared so much with Wentworth that in fact she came to share his very identity. As Wentworth recovered from his wounds, Nina filled the vital function of being The Spider's stand-in. More than that, she not only took over Wentworth's cloak and guns, but actually assumed the personality of The Spider.

Nina felt lead tug at her cloak and once more laughter rasped from her throat. She fired both automatics, and laughed to feel their bucking thrust against her slender wrists. The gunman was jerked up straight on his feet, hurled over backward by the powerful slugs that struck him. He rolled over twice before he lay still . . . She had slain—slain in the cloak and the name of The Spider!

It was not the last time Nina killed for The Spider. That Master of Men went on murdering for law and order into the forties, even after his creator went off to war. But time and paper rationing caught up with him in 1943.

I can still imagine him in action—along with his inspiration, The Shadow. (Phillip José Farmer speculates these two are even opposite sides of the same schizophrenic man.)

Perhaps there is a Valhalla for Pulp heroes. There, on another mission of justice, strides a knight clad not in armor of iron but in the bronze skin of Doc Savage, striding proudly through Pulpland. But though he walks along in the bright sunlight, he walks alone except for his own little band headed by Monk and Ham. True, off in the distance one can see the dust-raising horses of Buffalo Bill, Young Wild West, Jim Hatfield—the "Lone Wolf" of the Texas Rangers—and even the Lone Ranger (he made a few brief appearances as the hero of his own pulp). The sky itself is certainly filled over Pulpland—the biplanes of G-8 and his Battle Aces snarl in never-ending combat with the Fokkers of the Hun, even as Bill Barnes, Air Adventurer, zips by in a new streamlined model capable of *three hundred miles an hour!* John Masters—the Lone Eagle—and Captain Combat dive ever onward in their Spitfires, against the winged hordes of Nazi Germany. Higher still burn the rocket trails of Kim Kinnison, Curt Newton and Tony "Buck" Rogers (he first saw light in the pages of *Amazing Stories*).

But the sunny vistas of Pulpland are vacant except for the striding Man of Bronze. Everybody else lurks furtively in the darkness. Not only the villains—Wu Fang, Shiwan Khan, Herr Doktor Kruger, Doctor Death—but the heroes too are furtively slithering through the dingy back streets, the deserted warehouses and the penthouse. Captain Satan lurks in a doorway. The Black Bat crouches behind a rooftop chimney. The Phantom Detective edges along a wall. The minions of gangland are only partly responsible for their caution, for they know that in a now-abandoned office building labeled Street & Smith is secreted the Master of them all.

Mocking laughter lifts through the corridors as The Shadow once again expresses his satisfaction at his knowledge of men and his ability to master and manipulate them. And forever in the wake of laughter, trapped in a web of shadow, The Spider stalks, always claiming himself to be the "Master of Men," rapsodizing about the lavish "loyalty" of those he hardly knows, and then knowing they will betray him in an instant. On he creeps, bullets lodged in his brain and heart, his body an agony demanding release, his guns freely giving away what he seeks. Now the guns bark and here a pickpocket's skull shatters and there a cop's heart bursts and over yonder a hood tries to stuff his guts back inside. For that moment, The Spider is *almost* (but not quite) glad to be alive.

'THE SHADOW'S SEAL'

Anyone who received a message sealed with the sign of The Shadow had damned well better pay attention to it!

I sent and received a number of such messages as a kid, all of an urgent nature such as "Meet me in front of the American Theater at six-thirty." The leader of our group, my cousin Mary, an early advocate of Women's Lib, had obtained a set of seals from The Shadow Club. As commander-in-chief of the local post of the organization she adorned all her communications with this official seal.

The packet of seals ran out all too soon, and Mary resourcefully provided more by cutting up a copy of *The Shadow* Magazine, which at the time used three tiny views of the Master of Men's Minds —left profile, head-on, right profile—as a constantly recurring design to break up the text of the pages. A single copy of the magazine produced hundreds of tiny heads for all club messages.

I grew to love the pulp magazines in the years after this. In fact, my obsession with science fiction magazines in particular led to my becoming a writer. But I was born too late for the really great days of the pulps. The great characters— The Shadow, Doc Savage, The Lone Eagle—were on their last legs by the time I was really old enough to read them. *Doc Savage* and Lamont Cranston's journal were drab digest-size things in the middle forties. I was a grown man prowling through back-number stores before I saw a vintage issue of *The Shadow.* There he was, a big automatic in either fist, his black cape lifting in the wind like the sail of some Stygian vessel, its underside dipped in blood by a sinking sun that promised the mystery of night. (Just thinking about the pulps produces purple prose!)

Besides the pages dripping a figurative flood of crimson and purple, the old pulps also offered a lot of swell stuff I missed out on at the time but have observed in the troves of other collectors. Pulp heroes had premiums, even as radio heroes did. Badges were a prerequisite, of course. There was a Shadow badge in the image of those stickers previously mentioned.

The radio show of The Shadow also had premiums of its own during its decades of demonstrating that Lamont Cranston knew what evil lurked in the hearts of men. The broadcast version differed from the pulps in that The Shadow had the hypnotic power to cloud men's minds so that they could not see him, making him literally invisible. In the novels his black garb blended with the shadows of night to make him figuratively invisible, but not immune to the penetrating beam of a spotlight. The Master of Men's Minds did a lot more talking on the air, threatening and coaxing information out of suspects instead of merely banging away at them with his big automatics. The producers of the radio series had their own ideas about doing things, as revealed in their choice of premiums.

Actually, there was only one significant Shadow radio premium—The Shadow Blue Coal Ring. The band boasted a likeness of the cloaked Shadow on either side and a likeness of the sponsor's product on top—a lump of coal. The ring glowed in the dark—not the best jewelry for a man trying to hide in the shadows. There were a few other radio giveaways—an autographed photograph, a free blotter, compliments of The Shadow and Blue Coal—but they hardly count in the face of such a snazzy ring, generally considered the rarest and most valuable of all radio premiums, selling now for as much as $250.

The Master of Darkness' companion at the Street & Smith publishing empire, Doc Savage, offered another badge with his semi-profile in a bronze-appearing metal, totally fitting for the Man of Bronze. Besides his badge, Doc also sent you for your dime a certificate to sign, in which you agreed to uphold his previously cited code. The do-gooder formula sounded like a sure-fire way for getting yourself into trouble, and perhaps getting your nose punched for your unasked interference.

Some of the other magazines demanded more of you than money and human decency. To join the club of *G-8 and his Battle Aces* you had to get three others to agree to purchase the Master Flying Spy's magazine each month. (They became sort of apprentice members who could go out and try to round up three new readers on their own.) *The Lone Eagle* and *The Phantom Detective* had somewhat similar requirements for their clubs. The stipulation in all of these contracts was that each member had to "purchase his own magazine" each month. It must have been a forlorn hope that the fans would not share their copies of each issue, for those titles are all now out of business.

That Master of Men, The Spider, also had a club. He was a bit different (as usual) in offering a ring, not a badge. The ring bore his famous blood-red spider design to terrify lawbreakers and disgust mothers. At one point he offered a pencil whose cap could imprint the same spider design that the cloaked hunchback usually stamped on the foreheads of the corpses he had just slaughtered. In the original stories Richard Wentworth (The Spider's secret identity) had used a cigarette lighter with a secret compartment for stenciling stiffs, but while the offer was being advertised he dutifully switched to the mechanical pencil. (All too few of the readers were yet allowed to carry matches or a cigarette lighter.)

PULP PRICES

"Hero" pulps—magazines like *The Shadow, The Spider, Doc Savage, G-8 and his Battle Aces* and *Bill Barnes*—are the most valuable, with single issues from the thirties worth ten to fifteen dollars each, and occasionally more. First issues of the more famous titles are almost unavailable, but might be sold for thirty-five to fifty dollars on the occasions they show up. (In general, pulp collectors are more mature than comic book collectors and simply refuse to pay really fantastic amounts of money for copies.)

"Air War" titles—those without regularly continuing heroes, such as *Daredevil Aces, Wings,* etc.—are perhaps next in value, averaging about six dollars each.

Science fiction magazines are the most highly collected of all, but because they were saved by so many people they are very abundant. Twenty-year-old comic books can be quite valuable—the first issue of *Mad* is worth fifty dollars or more—but SF magazines from the same period are so common they are often worth no more than their cover price. Of course very old *Amazing Stories* and *Astounding* from the late twenties and the thirties can be quite expensive.

Weird Tales is a field of collecting all to itself. Almost any issue of that single magazine of ghosts and ghoulies is worth four or five dollars. Earlier ones are twelve to twenty dollars or more. The first issue from 1923 is an almost unheard-of rarity; perhaps only half a dozen copies are known to exist. (A selling price—perhaps by the widow of a collector—might be around five hundred dollars.) Other horror magazines—generally short-lived—such as *Terror Tales, Horror Stories,* and *Strange Stories* are also sought after at ten to fifteen dollars a copy.

Many collectors covet the mildly erotic magazines of the thirties (most of the eroticism was of the sado-masochistic type), which seem more quaint today than shocking. *Spicy* was the name of one particular line (although it is more or less generic today). There were *Spicy Detective, Spicy Mystery, Spicy Adventure,* even *Spicy Western.* These are now in the eight-to-fifteen dollar category, depending on age, condition and personal whim.

Routine Western or detective pulps are not highly sought after. A few Western titles such as *Wild West Weekly* or the above *Spicy Western* are collected, but the average Western pulp *(Ranch Romances, West, Big Book Western)* is simply not much sought after. Similar detective titles—*Double Detective, Smashing Detective, Thrilling Detective*—are in the same category. They remain on dealers' shelves forever. Fifty or seventy-five cents is the selling price. Adventure pulps of the *Argosy* type fare only a bit better. In general, in pulps as in comics, it is the element of *fantasy* which creates the desire to collect the magazines.

FANZINES

LIMITED EDITIONS WITH
UNLIMITED IMAGINATION

There have been amateur magazines in various fields such as poetry for many generations, but all the traditions of those in the general nostalgia field began with the science fiction fan magazines—popularly condensed to "fanzines." Shortly after Hugo Gernsback created the first professional science fiction magazines—*Amazing Stories* (still published after passing through many hands) in 1926, followed by *Science Wonder Stories*—fans began issuing the first amateur SF fanzines. *The Time Traveller* is often credited with being the first fanzine, although the matter is hazy and debatable. Many of the people behind the early fanzines have gone on to professional success—Jerry Siegel and Joe Shuster, creators of the *Superman* comic strip; Mort Weissinger and Julius Schwartz, executive-level comic magazine editors; Forrest J. Ackerman, Ray Palmer, and Sam Moskowitz, writers and editors in other fields.

A later generation brought writers such as Ray Bradbury into the fanzines. The author of *The Martian Chronicles* had his own fanzine in the forties, *Futuria Fantasia*, ten cents then, fifty dollars now. Famous science fiction fanzines have included *Fantasy Commentator, Spacewarp, Peon, Hyphen,* and *Psychotic*—names famous to only a few hundred people, but possessing a fame that survives by a kind of tribal memory among the small core of science fiction enthusiasts. (Many of these publications strayed far away from reviewing SF books and profiling authors as they became more concerned with fandom itself, the drinking and sex habits of other fans—occasionally detailed with memorable wit, but usually not.)

For decades, the *only* type of amateur magazine was the science fiction fanzine. Almost anybody could publish one. A whole edition could be put out for perhaps ten dollars. The standard means of reproduction was the hectograph—a tray of jelly-like substance that took an ink impression and passed it on to seventy-five copies or so—and the mimeograph, the stencil-type duplicator good for several hundred copies. Today, the standard procedure has become offset printing done to order in a print shop, which raises the price for a single edition of a fan publication to something like a few hundred dollars.

I put out my first fanzine when I was thirteen years old. A reader of the SF pulps since eight or nine, I had sent off for sample copies of some of the fanzines reviewed in the professional columns and had decided to lend my own efforts to the field after contributing a few articles here and there and occasionally striking up a correspondence with other fans.

To publish my magazine I laid out hard cash for a "press"—$2.95 for a postcard mimeograph. The gadget worked like a huge rubber stamp: you pressed the stencil surface down on the paper, rolled it back and forth, and lifted the stamper. Behold: a freshly "printed" page. At least that was the way it was supposed to work. Inking was only one problem among many.

I brought out two issues of a publication called *Asteroid X* using the device, even achieving two-color art. The contributors included my late dear friend, Bob Farnham, and the incredibly kind Ray Bradbury. Mostly, however, *Asteroid X* was a mess, and made no impact on the fanzine field.

Now, some years later, I am in my spare moments the associate editor of *Riverside Quarterly*, almost unanimously held to be the best current science fiction fan magazine, thanks to the editor-publisher, Leland Sapiro. My own contributions are limited to a column of rambling comment, but Lee Sapiro not only analyzes the early Gernsback era of SF deftly, but also rounds up other articles, verse and occasional fiction from the mainstay professionals and fans—Jack Williamson, Kris Neville, Bill Blackbeard, Poul Anderson and many others. The magazine is actually a continuation of *Fantasy Advertiser*, created by Roy Squires, which published the best articles in the field from the forties onwards. *Riverside Quarterly*, once published on Riverside Drive in New York, is now issued by Lee Sapiro at Box 40, University Station, Regina, Canada. This digest-size, offset-printed magazine, averaging eighty pages, costs 60¢ per copy, or four seasonal issues for two dollars. As you have probably guessed, it is purely a labor of love.

A RADIO FANZINE

Another fanzine of which I was editor-in-chief a few years back was called *Radiohero.* It was symptomatic of the subdividing of the fanzine field from an exclusive preoccupation with science fiction. Of course, virtually all my contributors and readers were SF fans in the beginning, but our subject matter was the old radio adventure serials. In its own way, *Radiohero* was astonishingly successful. It was the central subject of an article in *Life* magazine and was written up in several major newspapers. It earned me a chance to put on a radio series devoted to vintage broadcasts on the Pacifica network of FM stations, and it drew the attention of a publisher for whom I wrote a book called *The Great Radio Heroes,* followed by *The Great Radio Comedians,* both modest successes. In fact, the present work is an outgrowth of that mimeographed fanzine.

Nostalgia can be subdivided into some very specialized areas. Those people solely interested in collecting bubble gum picture cards do not represent a large enough potential audience to support a newsstand magazine such as *Time, Playboy* or *Field & Stream.* To my knowledge, there is not even a limited-edition magazine distributed by mail *exclusively* for gum card collectors, although they can find their wares advertised in *The Buyer's Guide for Comic Fandom.* There are many other small-circulation publications for other fields of nostalgic interest.

It might be easy to call these journals "amateur" magazines. The word is not entirely appropriate, however. Many of these publications do not look amateurish or read amateurishly in the least; moreover, many turn a quite professional profit.

COMICS FANZINES

In the early sixties, another fanzine appeared that apparently represented a larger group of readers. It was *Alter-Ego,* edited by Jerry Bails and Roy Thomas, the first significant comic book fanzine. From that start, hundreds more have appeared. They have ranged from incredibly elaborate projects costing five dollars a copy (and maybe worth it) to sloppy items far below the appearance and simple literacy of the lowest SF fanzine.

The norm at present seems to be elaborate offset-printed art portfolios, presenting the best work of amateur artists and usually the most casual work of the professionals like Frank Frazetta, Jim Steranko and Mike Royer, sometimes dashed off on the back of a menu at a convention for a quivering fan. These are one-shot affairs, coming and going at a frantic and profitable pace.

The most popular comic book fanzine seems to be *The Buyers Guide for Comic Fandom,* a a biweekly tabloid newspaper almost exclusively devoted to advertisements of fans and dealers trying to sell each other old and new comic books, mostly the Marvel line *(Captain America-Human Torch-Spiderman)* from the sixties and seventies, with an ever-diminishing supply of the "Golden Age" comic magazines of the forties. (Most of the older comics have now gone into the hands of collectors who are keeping them.) There are other ads for new fanzines and for comics fan conventions—there seems to be one going on virtually every weekend in the year some place in the country.

The minuscule nonadvertising content consists of peppy covers, a letter column and a comicland news column by Don and Maggie Thompson, once publishers of their own news magazine, *Newfangles,* now regrettably discontinued. The best thing about *The Buyers Guide* is that it is virtually free. Once sent out entirely without charge, it now costs two dollars for twenty-four issues a year—a mere 9¢ each. That price little more than pays for the postage and handling. The editor-publisher is Alan Light, a young man still in his teens with a keen business sense and a love of comic art. The address is DynaPubs, RR 1, Box 297, East Moline, Illinois 61244.

The forerunner to *The Buyers Guide* was *Rocket's Blast-Comicollector* (a combination of two magazines). From some unbelievably primitive hectographed issues, composed of faint purple smears, the magazine has become a professionally printed publication, at times running four-color covers in the manner of a newsstand publication. *Rocket's Blast* has a touch more of nonadvertising matter: on an average about ten of the magazine's 140 pages carry material other than ads. The primary editorial matter is a column of miscellaneous information by Howard P. Siegel.

The chief difference between *Rocket's Blast* and *The Buyer's Guide* is that the older publication is sold at a stiff price. A single copy of *Rocket's Blast* is one dollar by third class mail, $1.25 first class, or $1.50 air mail. (Fast delivery is important to collectors wanting to get their orders in first for any bargains.) Subscriptions are seven dollars for twelve monthly issues; twelve dollars first class; sixteen dollars air mail. This magazine claims 2,250 paid subscribers, while *The Buyer's Guide* reports 5,600. The advertising rates in both are modest—a full typewritten page can be reduced to a quarter of its original size (tiny but readable with effort) for around five dollars.

Both publications offer basically the same service. It was *The Buyer's Guide* which won a recent popularity poll. It was, however, the publisher of *Rocket's Blast* who pioneered this type of fanzine over many personal and financial handicaps. He is Gordon B. Love at The S.F.C.A., 9875 SW 212 St., Miami, Florida, 33157.

A word about the prices in the ads in these advertising fanzines. While I have already dealt with comic book prices in some detail, it should be noted that fans often sell their comics much more cheaply than a dealer would, to insure moving them. A dealer may ask sixty dollars for *Captain Marvel* No. 5, but a fan may be satisfied with ten dollars. Then, too, if you are not too fussy, fans often sell copies too beaten up or with too many pages missing for dealers to bother selling. That same *Captain Marvel* No. 5 with a couple of pages out might be only five dollars; without covers, only a few dollars. Of course, many fans want fully as much as dealers, and occasionally have ideas inflated beyond all reason.

Another influential comics fanzine, one containing something other than advertising, is *Graphic Story World,* a journal about "underground comix, comic books, animated films, books" with reviews and columns. The editor-publisher is Richard Kyle, who coined the term "graphic story." The new generic label has caught on to the extent that Kyle and his best friend use it among themselves all the time. While Kyle has a serious and intelligent interest in comic art, his favorite term seems too academic for a field that has always gotten down to basics. The old term "comics" does seem in danger of being replaced, but by the more informal "comix," which is properly applied only to underground panel art—mostly smut, trash and garbage, as its creators happily testify (some of it artistically executed, however). But the term is more and more being improperly applied to all comics magazines from *Donald Duck* to *Batman.*

Kyle's approach to the genre is less formal than his title might imply, but it is systematically structured. Author and artist profiles are mixed with news columns, letter pages, and samples of the comics discussed. A cosmopolitan atmosphere prevails, with much discussion of comics from France, Italy, Britain and elsewhere. Considering the probable lack of interest or exposure of readers to this foreign invasion of our hallowed shores, there is perhaps too much news from overseas. Nevertheless, *Graphic Story World* is the best single source of information on the comics field. It is available for 50¢ per copy, or six issues for three dollars, from Richard Kyle, P.O. Box 16168, Long Beach, California 90806. The 8½-by-11-inch offset-printed magazine, averaging thirty-two pages, is well worth the price.

There is another magazine with "Graphic Story" in the title. It is *Graphic Story Magazine,* edited and published by Bill Spicer, 4878 Granada St., Los Angeles, California 90042. (Kyle previously did a column of comment for this publication, coining the term which Spicer adapted for the title, changing it from *Fantasy Illustrated.)* Editor Spicer has taken this publication from being one of new comic book stories (too offbeat for commercial publication) to a series of in-depth profiles of significant comic artists, along with portfolios of their work. Some of these projects are magnificent and worth the price of a hardcover book and therefore they're a steal at $1.25. Past issues have presented the highlights of Will Gould, creator of *Red Barry,* a great detective strip of the thirties which was more realistic than *Dick Tracy* but more stylized than *Kerry Drake.* Another issue starred Basil Wolverton, whose meticulously drawn fever hallucinations have inspired Robert Crumb and countless other comix artists. Most of Spicer's special issues sell out their limited edition runs immediately, but no doubt new triumphs lie ahead.

Witzend is a curious "fanzine," since it is put together entirely by professionals. The great science fiction E.C.-group artist, Wallace Wood, is currently listed as "Founder" with Ed Glasser as publisher and Bill Pearson as editor. Naturally, since Wood is an artist, the magazine runs heavily to art, and to comic book stories which are too intellectual, too noncommercial—in short, *too good*—to be published in a newsstand comic magazine. But more than that, it publishes in-depth interviews with such giants of the field as Will Eisner, the man whom I regard as simply the best comic book artist-writer that there ever was. (Remember The Spirit prowling through garbage-laden alleys?) The magazine is roughly as tall and wide as *Playboy,* has fewer pages (and fewer ads), and sells for a dollar a copy from *Witzend*, Box 882, Ansonia Station, New York, N.Y. 10023.

The Menomonee Falls *Gazette* at first glance seems a rather conventional publication for a fanzine, but each week it publishes all six daily episodes of certain newspaper comic strips. Included are such nostalgic titles as *Tarzan, Johnny Hazard, The Phantom, Mandrake,* etc. These names sound nostalgic because it has been a long time since the reader of the average newspaper has seen them in print. A growing indifference to comic strips in general and to adventure strips in particular has caused many famous old titles to be dropped from so many papers that they are barely hanging on. Some strips are kept running in a half dozen American papers only because they are popular and profitable overseas.

The trouble with comic strips today is that many famous titles are kept going after the artists who made them famous have died. Trading on past glories, the present strip is often just plain awful. (A good example of awfulness is the current *Flash Gordon* in the *Gazette.*) A few strips show some style—witness Al Williamson's *Secret Agent Corrigan* (formerly *Secret Agent X-9).* Williamson's work on the present-day espionage feature is fine, but, curiously, he is the artist best suited to continue *Flash Gordon* in the great tradition of the late Alex Raymond, as he proved in a fine series of comic magazine *Flash Gordon* stories. Such is the way the minds of syndicate chiefs work that he is instead placed on the old *Secret Agent X-9* strip. Oddly enough, Alex Raymond worked on this same old chestnut before he began his classic voyage to the Planet Mongo. One can only hope that history might repeat itself. Meanwhile, Williamson's work can be followed along with that of Siegel and Shuster on the early, reprinted *Superman* and Burne Hogarth's re-run *Tarzan* in the *Gazette.* The paper is somewhat smaller than tabloid size and sells for 35¢ per copy, twelve issues for $4.50, from Street Enterprises, N85 W16505 Mary Ct., Menomonee Falls, Wisconsin 53051.

Some other comic fanzines of more than usual interest—with a similar makeup of artist profiles, character histories and art portfolios—are *Comicology,* 25¢ per copy, from Doug Fratz, editor-publisher, University of Maryland, Cumberland Hall E. Room 207, College Park, Maryland 20742; *Comic Fandom Monthly,* 50¢ per copy (suspended but back numbers available), from Joe Brancatelli, editor-publisher, 2016 E. 23 St., Brooklyn, N.Y. 11229; and *The Collector,* one dollar per copy, from Bill G. Wilson, editor-publisher, 1535 Oneida Dr., Clairton, Pennsylvania 15025. This last-named *Collector* covers not only comics but regularly has articles on old radio drama and radio box top offers.

Comic fanzines come and go, sometimes very swiftly, but the very first publisher in the field is still at it. Jerry Bails offers *The Collector's Guide to the First Heroic Age,* an elaborately designed, offset-printed booklet indexing every single costume character to appear in comic magazines from 1934 to 1947 for five dollars per copy. Lower-priced and less elaborate are his *Panelogist,* Volumes I, II, and III, 75¢ each from 487 Lakewood Blvd., Detroit, Michigan 48215. The last shall be first, and quite possibly Jerry Bails will still be dedicatedly digging up facts and figures on panel art when the rest of the world has let the comic strip fall back into total neglect.

MOVIE FANZINES

A multimedia fanzine is *The Jasoomian*, dedicated to Edgar Rice Burroughs and all his creations—especially Tarzan—in all their appearances in comics, radio, movies, hardcover books, magazines, and, one supposes, any stray images of the Ape Man that may have been picked up by telepathy. Recent issues have reported the death of Gene Pollar, the second screen Tarzan from silent days, complete with a reproduction of the funeral parlor leaflet handout, reproductions of letters from the late Mr. Burroughs, pictures of Tarzan toys, a facsimile of the dust jacket of a Tarzan parody novel published in Austria, the label of a Tarzan radio program transcription, etc. It is a fascinating case of monomania, available for one dollar per copy from the dedicated editor-publisher, William Dutcher, P.O. Box 1305, Yuba City, California 95991.

An all-movie-oriented fanzine, dedicated to a very special species of film, is *Those Enduring Matinee Idols. TEMI,* as it is called for short, is undoubtedly the most professional in appearance of all fanzines—be they science fiction, comics, movie or whatever. It is *Playboy*-size, set in real type (most fanzines merely reproduce typewriter copy) and replete with countless halftone photographs. The editorial standards and art layout are professional as well. Occasionally some of the writers cannot match their enthusiasm for old movie serials with flawless writing ability, but it doesn't seem to matter. What comes across is a love for a joyous part of childhood, the thrill-filled Saturday matinee. Editor Bob Malcomson and his staff and readers can identify every actor who walked across any frame of any serial ever made, name the person who composed each note of the musical score, and account for every cent spent in production and publicity. Occasionally they forget that these continued cinemas were *fun.* And what fun— *Flash Gordon, Dick Tracy, Zorro Rides Again, Perils of Nyoka,* on and on, until the last cliffhanger in 1956. You can remember along with them for only one dollar a copy or six bimonthly issues for five dollars, from editor-publisher Robert M. Malcomson, 38559 Asbury Park Dr., Mt. Clemens, Michigan 48043.

Fanzines have come a long way in professional appearance, as exemplified by *Matinee Idols,* and in intellectual standards, such as those of the *Riverside Quarterly,* from the often semi-literate, often illegible purple gazettes of the thirties. Some are even making a profit these days, and the field may become an established part of publishing. Fanzines these days are sometimes really prozines.

FROM FANZINES TO FANBOOKS

The same principles that apply to fanzine periodicals also describe a growing shelf of fan-published books. The finest examples of books published by a fan are those issued by Roy A. Squires from 1745 Kenneth Road, Glendale, California 91201. With a precise selection of type faces and textured paper, Mr. Squires produces a series of pamphlets, bound in parchment-like boards, hand-tied with cord. The editions are limited to around three hundred copies. The subject matter has consisted of verse, short stories, essays by H.P. Lovecraft, Clark Ashton Smith, Ray Bradbury and others. Two of those remaining in print are works of poetry by Robert E. Howard, *Black Dawn* (105 lines on 7 pages, limited to 234 copies) and *The Road to Rome* (54 lines on 6 pages, limited to 217 copies). The charge is $5 per copy— a high price, but worth it to admirers of Robert E. Howard and of fine bookmaking.

A man who has been publishing even longer than Roy Squires is William L. Crawford. Although still quite an active man, he has probably been publishing science fiction and fantasy longer than any other man in the United States. Only a few years after Hugo Gernsback began *Amazing Stories,* Bill Crawford brought out his own *Marvel Tales,* called a fanzine by some, a professional magazine by others. At any rate, it was not sold on newsstands and is a rare item today. After World War Two, when paper rationing eased up, Mr. Crawford began his Fantasy Publishing Company, Inc., issuing booklets such as *Garden of Fear* by Robert E. Howard, hardcover volumes such as *The Radium Pool* by Ed Earl Repp, and magazines such as *Fantasy Book* and *Spaceway* (the magazine where the present writer first got into professional print). Today Mr. Crawford is busy with his *Witchcraft & Sorcery* magazine, published in a limited edition rather like a fanzine but with professional standards. Many of his books and magazines, sold by dealers at high rates, are still in stock at cover price for mint, new copies from Fantasy Publishing Company, Inc., 1855 W. Main St., Alhambra, California 91801.

Fan publishing has lured diverse people from other fields. Kirk Alyn, the first actor to play Superman in the movie serials, has published his own book about those fabulous cliffhangers of the Man of Steel and the rest of his career on stage and screen. (Mr. Alyn should not be confused with the late George Reeves, TV's Superman.) Kirk Alyn's book has several hundred pages, dozens of photographs, a four-color cover. It is called *A Job for Superman* and autographed copies are available for $4.50 from Mr. Alyn at P.O. Box 1362, Hollywood, California 90028.

One of the finest artists to ever draw superhero comics, and in fact probably the best living comic book artist under thirty-five years of age—Jim Steranko—has started his own publishing company, based on the fanzine approach. Depending mostly on direct mail orders, Mr. Steranko has began a monumental *History of Comics.* It is published in huge paperback books the size of *Life* magazine. The first one, about Superman, Batman and the DC group as well as Captain America, Human Torch, Sub-Mariner and the Marvel group, is available for $3.25. The second, longer Vol. II is $5.40, and concerns Captain Marvel, Spy Smasher, Plastic Man, The Spirit and others, and contains special credits for Gill Fox, Jerry DeFuccio, Jim Harmon and Hames Ware. The covers by Steranko himself and inside illustrations by the original artists of the features involved are remarkable. Adding to his fan publishing empire, Steranko started a deluxe-fanzine, *Comixscene,* covering comics, films, underground comix, paperback and old pulps. It is tabloid-size, 50¢ per copy, 6 bimonthly issues for $2.50. Steranko is at Supergraphics, Box 445, Wyomissing, Pennsylvania 19610.

The present writer has answered requests from many readers of his books, *The Great Radio Heroes,* and *The Great Radio Comedians,* for more photographs of the actors who performed on *Tom Mix, Jack Armstrong, I Love a Mystery, The Shadow, Fibber McGee and Molly, Ma Perkins* and others. All these pictures were rounded up in a 40-page oversize paperback book, *The Pictorial Guide to Old Time Radio,* sold by mail for $2.50 from Jim Harmon, P.O. Box 38612, Hollywood, California 90038.

TV GUIDES

Do you remember when you grabbed *TV Guide* up off the newsstand and paged through it with excitement and anticipation? Part of the excitement then was merely the newness of the medium but, as with most of our wave of nostalgia, there is a bit more to it than that. The programs—and the audience—were fresher, and each show did not have to appeal to the same mass audience.

There were shows that said something to practically everybody: *I Love Lucy,* Milton Berle's *Texaco Star Theatre,* Jackie Gleason, and Sid Caesar and Imogene Coca in *Your Show of Shows.* There were also shows for children, right in prime time: *Kukla, Fran and Ollie, The Lone Ranger,* and *Sergeant Preston of the Yukon.* There were shows for people who liked to think: *Omnibus, Wide, Wide World, Opera Theatre.* In those days, people complained about these programs being segregated into an "intellectual ghetto" on Sunday afternoons. In answer to the complaints, the networks burned the ghetto down and moved in the *Amateur Hour.*

Many programs come back in memory unaided, but others are brought back through a haze of fringe-area interference by glancing through the pages of an old *TV Guide.*

In those old *TV Guides* you can spot beautiful color photographs of Clayton Moore as the Lone Ranger. What a pleasure it was to see your favorites in full color back then when you were used to seeing them in fuzzy gray tones on the tube. One of my biggest interests when TV came in was being able to see my favorites from radio on the screen. Mr. Moore did not quite live up to my mental image created by Brace Beemer's voice—what human being possibly could?—but Jay Silverheels was just about perfect as Tonto.

It was disappointing to find that the first Captain Midnight on television was only a goggle-helmeted announcer for Ovaltine, introducing re-runs of old movie serials of Zorro. On the other hand, the *Sky King* TV series was better written, acted and produced than the radio show—perhaps the only such adaptation I could say that about.

Of course, younger kids were introduced to brand-new shows made especially for the new medium. *Captain Video* was a live television show with much the flavor of old radio serials. (In fact, the title role was played by Al Hodge, who was the Green Hornet on radio.) The very earliest *Captain Video* shows were merely excuses to run old cowboy movies with Ken Maynard and others. The Captain and his Video Rangers would be off in space on some thin plotline, but they would tune in on one of his Video Rangers back on Earth to see how the cowboy was making out. Later, the show became all science fiction, written by Damon Knight, Richard Matheson and other gifted SF writers. It was still space opera, and a lot of scenes—such as the Saturnian space fleet battling the Alpha Centauri dreadnought—were merely described by Captain Video looking out a spaceport. The show was even merchandised like an old radio serial, with badges, rings, flashlight ray guns, and toys like the Captain Video rocket launcher set.

Another live afternoon show, *Howdy Doody,* was a way of life back then. I saw a bit of it while waiting for Captain Video to rocket into view.

Thankfully, I was not too old for Bob Clampett's *Beany and Cecil,* or Burr Tillstrom's *Kukla, Fran and Ollie.* Cecil and Ollie were dragons not even the bitter pill of growing up could slay.

Some individual TV broadcasts were almost events in one's life. Who does not remember—if he was "there"—the night Lucy's baby was born on TV, almost as it was happening in real life. Remember when Jackie Gleason fell and broke his leg? Or when Mary Martin flew as Peter Pan? Or Maurice Evans as Hamlet? (There was this shot of him looking into a hand-held mirror as he mused "To be or not to be . . . ," with the camera shooting over his shoulder into the glass. In my teens, knowing almost nothing of the technical aspects of films or television, I still wondered at the accuracy of getting that angle just right, so that the mirror did not pick up the camera behind him.)

Thumbing through those old digests jogs one's memory. You may remember Jack Webb's *Dragnet* without any trouble (indeed in re-runs you may be unable to avoid it), but it might take an article or a picture to make you recall *The Plainclothesman,* whose face you never saw because the camera acted as the eyes of the detective, letting you see things as he saw them. That show might remind you of another unseen face from early TV, the countenance of the always off-camera Mabel, wife of *Rocky King, Detective,* played by Roscoe Karns.

We all had our favorites, and *TV Guide* helped us to find them. Do people still mark their *TV Guides?* I know I used to. For me, a *star* meant a must-see: stay home for this. A *check* meant see this if you don't get a chance to go out, or if you feel like watching TV. A *circle* meant "maybe," depending on your mood and circumstances. A *triangle* meant see part of this. See the last half of *Steve Allen* after the end of the overlapping *Maverick.* Going through the *TV Guide,* carefully marking your choices, was a ritual, and I spent half an hour or so each week doing it.

And then, after the week was over, I threw away the *TV Guide.* Oh, I saved a few articles here and there, but not the whole issue. But some smart people did save the whole issue, every issue, and these are now among the new class of collector's items.

The first issue of *TV Guide* is now worth about fifty dollars. Who is to say that it will not go up in value? Copies drop rapidly in value for later numbers, but most issues before 1960 are now worth several dollars if you can find the right people. Only *Playboy* is worth more among magazines of the same vintage. (Copies of *Life, Time, Reader's Digest* and *Saturday Review* of the same period are virtually worthless—a nickel to a quarter each.)

It is, you must understand, only the national *TV Guide* that has obtained this collector's value. There used to be certain local competitors, dubbed *TV Log* or *TeleVision Record* or some such, but these are not highly sought after. In general, they offered a list of television shows by program title only, week after week, with one or two feature stories (often publicity handouts printed verbatim) and page after page of advertisements from local merchants. While not totally worthless, these publications lacked the detailed program information in the national *Guide* ("Tonight Ricky rushes Lucy to the hospital on a false alarm—or is it?") and the feature stories with photographs of our favorites. Dinah Shore looked just a shade less glamorous in a sharp photograph than she did on the screen, and even admitted as much in the story along with the pictures. Some stars looked even better in color portraits, it seemed—Shari Lewis, Hugh O'Brian, Perry Como, Lassie.

Color, excitement, romance, information—*TV Guide* was the best 15¢ worth of magazine since the days of *Spicy Detective* and *G-8 and his Battle Aces.* Today, for perhaps fifteen dollars or more, those *TV Guides* serve to remind us of the glamour of a medium that sometimes seems as lost and faraway as the dramas and comedy of vintage radio.

THE REST
OF
THE TRUNK

Wear One Of These
COMICAL MOTTO RINGS
LOTS OF INNOCENT FUN
PRICE 25 CENTS EACH

No. 8330 25c   No. 8331 25c   No. 8332 25c

No. 8327 25c   No. 8328 25c   No. 8329 25c

Say, fellows! Wear one of these Comical Motto Rings and watch the girls sit up and take notice. Each ring has a funny saying on it, as shown in the above illustrations. They are witty and amusing, cause lots of harmless fun, and they are not in the slightest degree objectionable. If you sometimes find it difficult, from diffidence or shyness, to get on friendly terms with the opposite sex, just display one of these rings and see if it does not smooth the way to a more familiar acquaintance and cordial friendship. Oh, yes! The girls buy them, too. The ring is made in platinoid finish, with the lettering on black enameloid background. Six different mottoes to select from, as illustrated above. Order by number. **PRICE 25 CENTS EACH, POSTPAID.**

Crystal Radio Detector 25c
COMPLETE WITH CRYSTAL
RECEPTION POSITIVELY GUARANTEED

This Detector is practically a radio in itself, as it is possible to get reception with it alone, provided you are within 25 miles of a broadcasting station (or up to 100 miles under very favorable conditions). All you need is an aerial and an ear phone and you are all set. It is completely assembled and wired, all ready for use. It has two posts, making connection much easier, also making it possible to make changes quickly. Everything complete, including the stand, crystal cup, arm with catwhisker and necessary screws, an ultra sensitive crystal of the finest grade, two terminals for wire connections mounted on handsome base—**EVERYTHING COMPLETE FOR ONLY 25 CENTS POSTPAID.** Every set tested and reception positively guaranteed.
No. 6590. CRYSTAL RADIO DETECTOR. Price Postpaid....... 25c

122

JOHNSON SMITH NOVELTIES

Their motto was "We're in Business for Fun." The Johnson Smith Co. is still in business, still selling many of the novelties that made them famous in the thirties and forties. Unfortunately, you can no longer get the item that offered the most fun—the Johnson Smith catalogue itself. True, they will still send you a booklet of under a hundred pages full of many fascinating items. But long gone is their mammoth 478-page catalogue, which came to you hardbound for a slight extra expense (it was 15¢ in 1947). Leafing through these pages turns up item after item that bring back memories—things sent for with dimes and quarters, and received far more promptly than box top offers.

COMICAL MOTTO RINGS

The slogans were "Don't Rush Me, Big Boy," "So's Your Old Man," "Will 'Ya, Huh?," and the most appropriate: "If You Can Read This, You Are Too Darn Close." The sentiments were similar to those kids sport on their sweatshirts today—except that today's sentiments are much more visible and their language much more explicit. Our finger-ring protest slogans were so tiny they were virtually invisible, yet we secretly felt we were thumbing our noses at propriety. All that for 25¢ each.

MIDGET BIBLE

It was a tiny book, the size of a postage stamp, 224 pages thick, and you could actually read it with the aid of a magnifying glass.

Even if you were somewhat less than devout, there was a certain fascination in having a book so small. I had half a dozen of them in various drawers and boxes. The prices ranged from 15¢ for a plain, black paper-covered edition to 50¢ for a genuine imitation leather-bound copy with gilt edges

I found possessing one of these midget Bibles particularly reassuring after seeing a movie in which Bela Lugosi demonstrated his antipathy to crosses and other religious symbols. While one was not often attacked by vampires in the territory around Southern Illinois, it did no harm to be prepared.

CRYSTAL RADIO SET

As a kid, I was always fascinated with miniatures—miniature Bibles, miniature comics, miniature radios. I thought the keenest thing in the world would be a pocket radio, one you could carry along with you wherever you went and be able to listen to *The Shadow* or *Jack Armstrong* anyplace.

Long before transistor sets came on the market, magazines frequently advertised pocket radios looking much like the pocket-size sets youngsters tote around today. The catch—not made clear in the ads—was that you had to listen to them through an earphone, and you had to ground them to something like a radiator or part of a telephone with a long wire and a spring clip, which made it a bit difficult to stroll down the street grooving on Benny Goodman. What's more, these so-called pocket sets were usually outrageously priced at $7.95 or so.

Once again, Johnson Smith was in there with a crystal set costing only 35¢. The only problem was that you had to buy an earphone for $1.25. And the earphone was of the bulky diaphragm type, like the earpiece of a telephone. (This was before the simpler, inexpensive inner-ear contact type came along.) Eagerly, I sent in my money. Finally, my 35¢ radio came. After much, much experimentation, I found it actually worked. Strains of music came through—but not very often. I was too far from the nearest radio station, stuck in the prairie of Illinois. But good old Johnson Smith had not failed me—only the F.C.C. or the broadcasters of America or somebody. For a city kid, the crystal set must have been a great 35¢ investment.

THE VENTRILO

One of the Johnson Smith's most famous offers, in their catalogue and in countless comic book advertisements, was the Ventrilo. Some of the copy ran "Imitate Radio Favorites! Throw your Voice—into a trunk, under the bed, anywhere. Fool teacher, policeman or friends!" For only 12¢ you received this magical device and a 32-page booklet on ventriloquism. Alas, it was a shuck. The Ventrilo was a fiber disc of some kind you slipped under your tongue. You could use it for making vibrating, trilling noises like birdcalls—but other than that, the Ventrilo was not much good for anything but making your tongue sore. No, I could *not* throw my voice like Edgar Bergen. I could *not* throw my voice upstairs, downstairs, into a closet, up my pants leg and out my vest. My tongue got sorer and sorer. But then, it was only 12¢, and it was worth that just for the fun of imagining all the tricks I could play, throwing my voice out the window, through the door, up the chimney, into the basement, up my sleeve and out the hood of my yellow oilcloth raincoat.

PLANS FOR BUILDING ONE- AND TWO-PASSENGER AIRPLANES

For 25¢, Johnson Smith would send you a booklet that would tell you how to construct either a one-seat or a two-seat airplane (your choice) and then give you a course in how to fly it. They managed to do it all in 64 pages, too. On examining the booklet, one finds that it has several unadvertised bonuses—plans for building a glider and other plans for constructing a seaplane, *plus* sure-fire instructions on becoming an airline pilot. However, if one reads the fine print one finds several disclaimers such as "Let's be frank... it is doubtful whether any person not acquainted with aviation in most of its phases can successfully build his own plane."

While not thoroughly acquainted with *all* aspects of aviation, even though I had listened to *Captain Midnight* lots of times, I nevertheless considered building my own ship. The trouble was I could not make heads or tails out of the diagrams and blueprints. (Of course, I was only nine years old.) Looking at these diagrams as I write this, I realize that they make even *less* sense to me now than when I was nine. I don't think I want to wait any longer to smarten up. Does anybody want to buy a book on building your own airplane?

LIVE BABY ALLIGATOR

There was a Livestock Department at Johnson Smith & Co., stocked by the same guy who selected the Whoopee Cushion and Joy Buzzer. One of the prize offerings was a "Live Baby Alligator." The advertisement ran: "Alligators are actually very interesting pets that have been trained to do some amazing things." (Like eating people you don't like, one supposes.) "The Indians used to hypnotize them. Others have made them sing and laugh."

I thought it *would* be pretty keen to have a singing alligator around the house. It sounded like a heck of a lot more fun than a new kitten. While the alligator was only eighteen inches long, the illustration showed the little devil growing by stages—growing, growing, growing . . . finally rising up on its hind legs, a real monster! They were only $3.95 each, shipped direct from Louisiana.

In recent years, I have heard that what you really got was not an alligator but an alligator-like creature known as a caiman, sharp-fanged and bad-dispositioned. Personally, I suspect that what you got depended on whether alligators or caimans were cheaper that season. Not too many years ago, the *New York Times* ran a story about the sewers of New York City being filled with full-grown alligators—alive, devouring rats and cats. They had been flushed down the toilet after a certain length of time during which they flunked out as household pets. It's a good story.

I prefer to think you did get a real alligator. Of course, my folks would never let me send for one. If I had, he would probably be walking around on his hind legs by now. He would have had a lot of time to practice his singing. I could have been his manager and gotten him a job as the lead singer with a rock group. I blew the whole bit.

JOY BUZZER

(*Hand Shaker and Tickler*)

FUNNIEST JOKER'S NOVELTY EVER INVENTED!

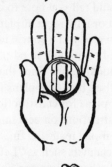

🖙 Use the ring as a key to wind it.

Wear it as a ring —the Buzzer in the palm. 🖙

🖙 It "shocks" them when they shake hands.

It makes them jump if they are ticklish. 🖙

🖙 They will hit the ceiling if they sit on it.

Under a sheet it feels like a mouse. 🖙

With one of these little contrivances you may have no end of fun. Attached to one end of the Joy Buzzer is a brass ring that slips over the second finger, allowing the Buzzer itself to be concealed unobserved in the palm of the hand. Inside the Buzzer is a clock-work mechanism that is wound up. Projecting from the center of the Buzzer is a brass point, and a little pressure upon this point releases the mechanism. Shake hands with someone and see the shock the person receives when he unconsciously releases the mechanism of the Buzzer. If he is ticklish, watch him jump. Place it on a chair and watch the commotion when someone sits upon it. Place it under a pillow—under a sheet it feels like a mouse. You can use it as an ordinary "tic-tac" on a door or window—use it to awaken a sleeper by holding it on the sole of the foot or just behind the ear—try it on the window of an automobile just as the gears are shifted; they will think the engine is "busted." Dozens of other uses will suggest themselves to you. It is well and strongly made, entirely of metal, and it is certain you will get more than your money's worth of fun out of this little contraption.

No. 2955. JOY BUZZER. Price Postpaid...................................... **28c**

JOHNSON SMITH & CO.

126

PRACTICAL JOKES

In my journey through life I have met a number of people who had all the class of a Whoopee Cushion. This delightful little object was inflated with air, and whenever your victim sat down in it the air was forced out with a sound like *"Brrraaaakkkk . . . ."* As the ad put it, "The results can be imagined."

Another delightful item was the Electric Joy Buzzer. It wasn't really electric, it just had a spring-driven device that unwound furiously to give a pronounced tickling sensation. "It 'shocks' them when they shake hands," the advertisement explained. "They will hit the ceiling if they sit on it." Not only that, but "Under a sheet it feels like a mouse."

You could also buy "Red Hot Gum—Makes Their Mouth Feel as if It Were on Fire!" For other small sums you could pick up a Lapel Squirt Badge, an Imitation Joke Rat, a Dribble Glass, Itching Powder ("It Drives 'Em Crazy!") and Stink Perfume.

I must confess I never sent for or used any of this stuff, which may be one reason I am still alive to write this. The closest I ever got to any of it was a "Glass & Plate Smasher"—six metallic plates that sounded like breaking glass when dropped. They did sound very convincing, and I got a few starts out of family members with them. I was mainly interested in them as a sound effect for the ad lib radio shows I was always rehearsing. Jules Feiffer writes of having muttered to himself in bed at night, doing his own radio shows, but I scripted mine, read them out loud and applied whatever sound effects I could muster. Come to think of it, I should have sent for a Whoopee Cushion. It would have made a great sound effect.

LIVE CHAMELEON

I never was allowed to order a pet alligator, but I did order a pet chameleon. The trouble with the whole idea, of course, is that you just can't get too chummy with a lizard. Dogs and cats and rabbits are warm-blooded, furry, and cuddly, while alligators, chameleons, turtles, and snakes are cold and scaly. Survival in nature to the contrary, in a home they just don't make it. But apparently in my era every kid had to find that out for himself.

According to Johnson Smith, chameleons changed color when they crawled over surfaces of varying hues. I could never detect this fabled change. Mine always looked greenish-gray from the time I took it out of the box it came in, a cardboard affair with holes punched in it. I had a color-blind chameleon. So you are nine or ten years old and you have this four- or five-inch long lizard that stays greenish-gray. "They feed themselves by eating small insects from the air," the ad claimed. That much must have been true. It never seemed to eat any of the special chameleon food that came with it. (If they fed themselves, why send extra food?)

You could fasten it by a tiny chain and collar to your lapel and *wear* your pet everywhere. I tried it. But people look at you funny when you go around with a lizard stuck to the front of you. More than that, you *feel* funny. I wouldn't say that I was *afraid* of the thing, but I did not exactly feel chummy toward it, like I did toward my dog.

One day, not while wearing it, the chameleon finally did something interesting. It escaped. With a super-reptilian leap, it cleared the sides of the cardboard crate where I kept it and was loose in the house. My mother took it as I expected her to take it—she screamed and told me to get that lizard out of her house.

I did my best to comply. I looked behind chairs, under chairs, underneath chair cushions. Next, I checked out the beds—looking under them, behind them. Pat down all the wrinkles to be sure the chameleon was not tunneling through the sheets. The thin wail of an outraged mother in the background really did nothing to aid my efforts. Desperately, I searched the shadows in the corner, and around the bookcase for the furtive gleam of tiny reptilian eyes. I did all this and more, but it was no use. My chameleon had disappeared. Finally, my mother's protests even wound down.

I spent a few restless nights. What could a five-inch reptile do, loose out there in the darkness? Yet, despite my uneasiness, nothing ghastly happened. None of us was attacked in our sleep. No gaping holes were chewed in the doors.

As winter wore on, every few weeks—sometimes every month or so—we would catch sight of the chameleon slithering out from under the dresser and going into the shadows beneath the bed. We could never catch it. Finally it was spring, and the doors were open to the brassy sunlight, the air still a bit snappy and free from insects. Then one afternoon we saw the chameleon slither out from under the sideboard (remember those?), go skipping across the porch, and take a great leap into a patch of sunflowers. We never saw it again. But considering its stamina and ability to "feed itself out of the air," the creature is probably still alive somewhere in our old yard.

Johnson Smith said its chameleons were worth 50¢ in 1948. They still sell them. My advice is not to buy one.

Johnson Smith never seemed to throw anything out or discontinue any item. The latest catalogue I have still offers items, especially booklets, which they were selling in the thirties. (The books are not reprints; the paper shows signs of yellowing.) I am reasonably certain you can *right now* still buy a copy of *Chorus Queens, or Lives of Hotcha Chorus Girls* (15¢ a couple of years ago). "This book contains 11 thrilling chapters, more than you would get in some books two or three times the size." If the quantity of chapters—some, no doubt, containing many sentences and several paragraphs —was not sufficient to induce you, the quality of the material should: "Intimate secrets and fascinating pastimes in the lives of famous Broadway hotcha girls." I imagine some of the many fascinating pastimes included are knitting, baking cookies, and miniature golf.

The Johnson Smith Co. is still in Detroit, Michigan (sufficient mailing address). I'm sure every day their employees drive up in their Model T's, come in and take off their celluloid cuffs and get right down to work mailing out all the Joy Buzzers, Ventrilos, Joke Rats, and Thurston Magic Books. I don't know if any of the items they sell have become great collector's items, since so many can still be purchased new, although some fast operators may be trying to pass off newly purchased items from the company as rare antiques. I do know that their catalogues themselves are valuable. The old Johnson Smith catalogue of almost 500 pages, long discontinued, can bring up to twenty-five dollars a copy. It is well worth it, no doubt, but I'm glad I still have the one I paid 15¢ for.

CHARLIE McCARTHY DOLLS

I knew Charlie McCarthy was not a real boy
when I was a kid. He was, I knew, just a wooden
doll that could talk. That was a lot better than
being a real boy. Charlie was not the only wooden
doll I knew about that could talk. There was also
Mortimer Snerd and some dummies in the movies
who were trying to do Charlie's act, but Charlie
was the only talking doll that really counted.
Charlie had found an ideal place to do his thing—
on the radio. Every Sunday night *everybody*
listened to the Charlie McCarthy show. When
Orson Welles presented his celebrated "Invasion
from Mars" (or, properly, *The War of the Worlds)*
in a time slot opposite Bergen and McCarthy one
night in 1938, the panic was limited to a few
thousand hotheads because—as one theory has
it—all the intelligent people in the country were
listening to Charlie McCarthy.

I guess I liked it best when Charlie talked back
to grown-ups—the schoolmasterish Edgar Bergen
or the pompous old drunk, W.C. Fields. Through
the static of the years, I remember exchanges
like these. . .

FIELDS: Well, well, Charlie McCarthy, my
    little pal. I've missed you. Been carrying
    the torch for you.
CHARLIE: I can see it on your nose.
FIELDS: Bright little nipper. That a new paint
    job he has there, Edgar?
CHARLIE: If I had a wick on me, I'd stick
    it in your mouth and rent you out as an
    alcohol lamp.
FIELDS: Is it true your father was a gate-leg
    table?
CHARLIE: If it is, your father was under it!
You could talk like that to grown-ups if your
head was made of wood. In some ways, dolls had
it better than people.

Some experts say all children of both sexes are
fascinated by dolls and actually retain that
fascination all their lives. Boys had lead soldiers,
and now have G.I. Joes, while girls used to play
with Shirley Temples and now dress Barbies.
Even when girls grow up they frequently decorate
their apartments with dolls or stuffed animals.

The guys grow up and, if they have enough money, furnish their dens with hitching-post boys from old Southern mansions, wooden Indians or Colombian figures. If they have less money, maybe they just have a Raquel-shaped pillow on the convertible sofa.

According to the paperback psychology books, girls are play-acting to learn how to be mothers. I suppose boys could be play-acting to learn how to be fathers, but I know that there is more to it than that. Dolls are people we can push around. We can put them in their place, while the rest of the world is putting us in ours. They are friends who don't have the initiative to go out and find somebody more interesting than we are, leaving us all alone. *I'd rather have a paper doll to call my own than a fickle-minded real live gal,* the Ink Spots used to sing.

The first Charlie McCarthy doll I had—perhaps when I was four years old—was a carnival prize.

The Wabash County Fair always smelled of sun-hot grass, manure, and fish sandwiches fried up by a local man, Punch Rogers. The Harmon family was there, walking the midway of tent shows, Ferris wheels, merry-go-rounds, and the prize pitches. My mother wore a new blue print dress, bought with money earned from selling peaches from our backyard trees. My father wore a white shirt with a clip-on bow tie and broad-brimmed straw hat. With his lean face and white mustache he looked old enough to be my mother's father (and, in fact, he *was* that old). Album portraits from this time show me wearing a sailor suit, vaguely like the kid on the Crackerjack box.

I saw Charlie on a rack above the ring-toss game, along with Betty Boop and Popeye and even a Lone Ranger. But Charlie was the one I wanted. I listened to the Bergen-McCarthy radio show every Sunday, and of course I had seen Charlie's picture many times in either the *St. Louis Post-Dispatch* or the *Chicago Tribune* rotogravure sections. This figure of Charlie was made of plaster of paris, colored wrong: he had a yellow tux and a red silk topper. I asked my father to get him for me.

"You can't buy the prizes, mister," the pitchman told my father. "You got to win 'em. Three hoops for fifteen cents. Two out of three go down over the target, you get something off the shelf. All three go down, you get something off the table." The table was the target area, and had cameras and wrist watches and bottles of perfume on white wooden blocks. The tossed hoop had to go down flat on the table around that white square.

My father, expert at horseshoe pitching, bought fifteen cents' worth of hoops and made three ringers, except that the rings did not quite sit flat on the table—they hung up on the corners a bit. My father bought another chance, and tossed more carefully. This time the first hoop went down *plop* over a camera, the next down *smack* over a pair of field glasses, and the last went *thunk* over a bottle of perfume. The pitchman went over to the table and pressed on the last hoop, making it go *click* as it hit the table. "Don't count if you can hear 'em click. They ain't down all the way then, mister."

"If they fit so tight you have to push the hoops down to make them hit the table, *nobody* could toss them over," Dad told the man.

"You looking for trouble, mister?" the pitchman asked, his face getting wet with sweat. That was not a good question to put to my father, who resembled in many ways the Western hero of a Saturday matinee (naturally, at the time I thought all fathers did and that there was nothing unusual in this). I'm not exaggerating when I say that when my father was well into his seventies he could chin himself fifty times—on a tree limb seventy-five feet in the air. He could drive nails into a fence post with revolver fire from twenty paces. The beer-bellied pitchman was not worrying him.

"Anything wrong, John?" a new voice interjected before Dad could answer. This man, taller and heavier than my father, was our local sheriff, Mr. Mobley. He wore no badge but the authority of his person.

"No trouble," my father said. He faced the suddenly sullen-faced pitchman. "You already have thirty cents of my money. I'll give you a quarter more for the statue for the boy."

The carnival man shrugged. "Okay. They only cost us about fifteen cents."

All during the rest of the Fair—watching trotting races, eating cotton candy (and those fish sandwiches), and going on the tamer rides—the Charlie McCarthy plaster doll was clutched under my arm.

When I got Charlie home, of course, I began doing my own ventriloquist act with him. I couldn't quite get the knack of throwing my voice, or even talking without moving my mouth, but I kept trying. One day Charlie slipped out of my hands as I was sitting on the back porch swing, and his head shattered on the floor. I wasn't completely destroyed by the tragedy. I hadn't been able to give him quite the personality that Edgar Bergen did, and he was not yet quite real to me.

My mother gathered up the pieces and told me Charlie could be fixed—all it would take would be some glue. But somehow she or my father never got around to getting the special glue it would take to repair the head, because it was actually *not* repairable. The body and the pieces were on a shelf for several years, it seems—perhaps it was only months—until at last I decided his case was terminal and dispatched the remains.

That was not the end of my fascination with Charlie McCarthy, however. I saw him wise-cracking, putting grown-ups in their places, and even walking around in several movies. Chase and Sanborn coffee made an offer, on their radio show and in the newspaper comic sections, of a cardboard figure of Charlie—hardly more than an animated paper doll, but his jaw was articulated. Naturally, I pestered my mother into sending for it. Eventually, I lost my Charlie McCarthy cardboard doll too. He just disappeared—misplaced, thrown out with the trash, swiped. Somehow he was gone.

About this time I got hung up on my new pearl-handled Gene Autry cap gun. I wish I could say for the benefit of all the anti-violence people that instead of becoming a nice, mild-mannered individual, I became a bank robber, thrill killer, or policeman, but that didn't happen either. The gun was just something else to use at play. I guess most adults can't remember that children really do not take play all that seriously. To them, it is just sort of *play*.

When, as an adult, I started collecting some of the alleged trivia of childhood I recalled the various Charlie McCarthys I had had. Neither of the two previously described has turned up in duplicate, but in one store I found a satisfactory surrogate. It is a Charlie McCarthy hand-puppet (circa 1939) with his tux reproduced in cloth and a head of regular doll-stuff, whatever that is. This Charlie is draped over an inverted drinking glass on my mantel, peering at all comers through his monocle. While he may not impress my friends as much as a stuffed Snoopy or a Raquel-shaped pillow, he seems a faithful sentry to help guard me against the assaults of Future Shock.

I have never actually tried making this Charlie speak. Perhaps some day I will take him around to the office of a certain Mr. Edgar Bergen, who conducts business just a few blocks from my apartment in Hollywood. Perhaps he could instill a spark of his magic in this Charlie—but then, I suppose, Charlie would never shut up.

(There are many different toy models of Charlie McCarthy, in various sizes, some sitting in chairs, some driving cars, valued at from ten to a hundred dollars, depending on age and condition.)

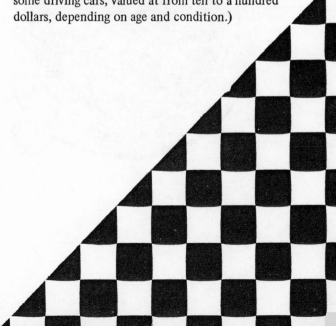

TOM MIX

PETER LORRE

"BLONDIE FOR VICTORY"

Playing in

A Columbia Picture

PENNY SINGLETON · ARTHUR LAKE

At "BILLY THE KID"   ★   A PRC Picture

Buy War Stamps for Victory

BUSTER CRABBE

"FORBIDDEN TRAILS"

Playing in

A Monogram Picture

THE ROUGH RIDERS

132

DIXIE CUP LIDS

The lid on the ice cream cup was round. On the top it said something like "Meadow Gold Ice Cream/Vanilla/4 fl. oz." But it was the underside you were interested in. The first glimpse of the mysterious underside (as distant as the other side of the moon unless you had a nickel to buy the ice cream cup) was clouded, mysterious. A paper coating covered the picture, keeping a movie star's face out of the vanilla. The outline of a ten-gallon hat told you it was a cowboy star, but you couldn't tell yet just which one. With excruciating care—you could accidentally peel off part of the picture if you messed up—you removed the waxed liner. And there was your circular picture of a cowboy great—Ted Weems! *Ugh!* Ted Weems, the orchestra leader who played second lead in some Johnny Mack Brown Westerns. Even when you were eight years old, you suspected he paid the movie studio to let him do it. Why couldn't it have been Johnny Mack Brown himself, or Wild Bill Elliot or a group shot of the Rough Riders (Buck Jones, Tim McCoy and Raymond Hatton), or somebody else? You sighed and shoved the Dixie Cup lid into your back pocket. At least he was a cowboy, sort of. It was better than a Bette Davis. That would have been completely worthless, not even worth taking home.

Despite a few misfires, it was a good deal. For a nickel you got a cup full of ice cream, with the movie star picture thrown in for free. The ice cream was made with real cream, not a bunch of exotic chemicals, and you got a quarter of a pint,

as I recall. (A pint of ice cream cost 15¢, so one did pay a bit more, but the movie star portraits were definitely worth the difference.) All those delightful, melting scoops with a wooden paddle on a July afternoon!

Bill "Hopalong Cassidy" Boyd, Gene Autry, and Don "Red" Barry were "valuable," but the most highly prized were the ones showing Buster Crabbe in his role as Flash Gordon from the movie serials. I do not know for certain if there ever was a portrait of Charles Middleton as Ming the Merciless, but there should have been. He was so masterly a villain that, like Fu Manchu, he sometimes seemed to be the real star of the stories.

Next to these serial favorites, the cowboys were most popular. Besides the well-known cowboys mentioned earlier, some horse opera stalwarts like Ken Maynard and Hoot Gibson used to turn up a lot, too. They were almost completely unknown to me. (This was before all of them made comebacks in the mid-forties.) It may have been old finding such old-timers when *I* was a boy, but a younger friend of mine tells me they were still using the same photographs of Buck Jones and the rest on ice cream lids when *he* was a boy during the mid-fifties!

The roundness of the lids probably contributes to their rarity today. They did not "save" well. They did not stack easily or keep neatly in a box. A round box would have been perfect, but unfortunately the lids wouldn't fit into one of the cups they covered. I know of no one who has a really extensive collection of them today, although you find them in some general collections of nostalgia and occasionally see them for sale in a sell-out of items found dumped in an old trunk. The going price is a couple of bucks each (without the ice cream, yet).

The name Dixie Cup, by the way, comes from the brand name of the container, which was printed fairly boldly on the product. Although it was the Meadow Gold Creamery that packaged the ice cream in the cups in my part of the country, I never heard anyone ask for a Meadow Gold cup. Indeed, I once knew a man who was district manager for Lily Cups. He was complaining to me about how Dixie Cups had so much of the market sewed up. "It isn't fair," he said. "Our Dixie Cups are better than theirs!"

JEAN HARLOW

RADIO'S SENSATIONAL CHILL SHOW...NOW ON THE SCREEN!

COLUMBIA PICTURES
presents

"I LOVE A MYSTERY"

with

JIM BANNON · NINA FOCH · GEORGE MACREADY · BARTON YARBOROUGH · CAROLE MATHEWS · LESTER MATTHEWS

Based upon the popular CBS radio program "I LOVE A MYSTERY" · Screen Play by Charles O'Neal
Produced by WALLACE MacDONALD · Directed by HENRY LEVIN

ROLAND WINTERS
AS
CHARLIE CHAN
in
Docks of New Orleans

with VIRGINIA DALE
MANTAN MORELAND
JOHN GALLAUDET · VICTOR SEN YOUNG

Produced by JAMES S. BURKETT · Directed by DERWIN ABRAHAMS · Screenplay by W. Scott Darling · Suggested by Earl Derr Biggers' character

134

MOVIE POSTERS

What promised more future delights than the posters outside movie theaters in the thirties and forties? If you needed any inducement to go inside (I didn't), the poster melted away all resistance.

Around the banner title "I Love a Mystery" were heads of a bearded, mysterious old duffer; the cool, lovely Nina Foch (promising romantic involvement); and a tough-looking character in a broad-brimmed hat (Barton Yarborough as one of the heroes, Doc Long); and over on the right-hand side a disfigured, one-eyed menace, suggesting a monster who was at least a distant relative of Karloff or Lugosi. Even if you were less familiar with the radio thriller than I was, the 11 x 14 poster—properly a lobby card—for the movie version would have made you step up and pay your twenty cents for a ticket.

I was always drawn immediately to the cowboy pictures of Gene Autry and Buck Jones, but other posters offered something for everybody. The drawing of a sedan crashing through a bridge guard rail hinted at Saturday matinee serial thrills. The names of stars like Jim Bannon and George Macready may have lured customers (Alice Faye or Tyrone Power proved even more effective on other posters). A famous title, established names, mystery, romance, horror, action! Who could resist?

You did not have to search long for thrilling scenes on the Western posters. There was always a big "head" of the star, usually making him look dignified, like a teacher or your father. But there was also a smaller shot of him on his horse riding like a bat out of h-ll. Still smaller views showed the hero hitting some fat guy so hard that the villain's back was arched like a bow. In another sketchy drawing the hero was getting it pretty good himself, with a chair being broken over his skull. There was usually a small photo of the hero's sidekick (most often Smiley Burnette) playing a guitar (but who cared about the music?)

There was one kind of poster I never saw in my home town of Mount Carmel, Illinois. That was a poster for the current serial showing at the local theater. I did not see one of those until I was in my twenties, when the publisher of the movie magazine I was working for showed me some of these "one-sheets," as they are called. There they were—Captain America in his red-white-blue uniform ready to pounce upon some evil-doers; Nyoka in her tailored khaki outfit drawing back from a sword-wielding Arab; Buck Jones, Dick Foran and the rest of the *Riders of Death Valley* galloping fearlessly into danger. If I had ever seen these as a kid I would have clawed them off the wall to get them.

For years I kept a scrapbook of all the serial advertisements in our local paper. These used no display mats, just the words announcing "The greatest serial of all time—Jack Armstrong!" Sometimes there would only be the word "serial," but I saved that, too.

Many adults today seem to feel the same way as I did then. Movie posters are highly sought-after items, available through many mail order dealers. A Texas millionaire has reportedly paid as much as a thousand dollars for an original William S. Hart poster, apparently being unaware that with a little looking one could find such a Hart poster for about a hundred dollars. Generally speaking, a hundred dollars is the maximum a movie poster might reasonably be expected to sell for. The average price for a poster for a film from the forties would be five to ten dollars. Posters for any film from the last three or four years can be found for around $1.50.

The most actively collected poster subjects are the genre films—Westerns, horror, crime. Of course, there is always the person who seeks one particular star—for instance, posters for the movies of Humphrey Bogart, Marilyn Monroe, or John Wayne. The silent movie posters are the rarest of all, because of age if nothing else. The thousand-dollar figure may be legend, but two hundred dollars might well be paid for a poster of Doug Fairbanks in *The Thief of Bagdad.* (Of course there are also the rare and valuable unusual items. A life-size color cardboard figure of Betty Grable with a fixed brace, a "standee," might sell for fifty dollars. A twenty-foot hand-painted canvas banner for the *Captain Marvel* serial might fetch that much or more.)

Originally, most of these posters came from film and poster exchange services, designed to serve theaters around the country. A few collectors found these exchanges and bought old posters advertising films that seldom if ever played theaters any more. Ten years ago—even

five—one could buy classic posters for 35¢ each, or crates of the stuff for five or ten dollars. But no more. All of those posters fell into the hands of collectors, book stores, and the like; Old posters are sold or traded only at premium rates these days. Many book stores dealing in such nostalgic paper goods as old comic books, movie fan magazines and the like also know what price to put on movie posters. If you want to pay their price, check the dealer directory elsewhere in this book.

What do people *do* with the posters once they get them? In general, they post the posters—in the living room or the den (depending on the wife's permissiveness). In general, poster collectors follow the same relentless, often unreasoning desire of all collectors—to save. They save and cherish something they love, something the more "normal" person would throw away as a worthless piece of junk.

CARL LAEMMLE *presents*

KEN Maynard

"WHEELS of DESTINY"

JOHNNY WEISSMULLER

"SWAMP FIRE"

VIRGINIA GREY
BUSTER CRABBE
CAROL THURSTON

Directed by WILLIAM H. PINE
Original Screenplay by Geoffrey Homes
A PARAMOUNT PICTURE

Savage with excitement!
Roaring with adventure!
Blazing with romance!

TOY GUNS

THE RED RYDER DAISY AIR RIFLE

If you were a kid during the forties, everywhere you looked you saw an advertisement trying to sell you a Red Ryder Daisy Air Rifle. Not that *you* really needed to be sold, but you were induced to put an ever-increasing amount of pressure on your parents to get you the B-B gun for Christmas or for your birthday. Some of the ads even offered you propaganda kits—stickers to put on your dad's shaving mirror saying "Remember, Dad—I want a Daisy!"

That "Reminder Kit" ad and others of a similar nature were on the back of about half of the comic books published. (The other half all seemed to have ads for Charles Atlas's muscle-building course.) They all showed Red riding his big black horse, Thunder, carrying his Daisy carbine. Sometimes there was a close-up of Red's craggy face, with him saying, "Remember—it's a Daisy!" Often there was a smaller picture of Little Beaver affirming, "You betchum, Red Ryder!" The price was only $2.95 in pre-World War Two days, and today it still looks like a handsome weapon.

I never had a Red Ryder carbine, but I did have a Daisy air rifle that I *wished* was a Red Ryder carbine. What was the difference? About a buck and a half—enough to a family on our income. I had the cheapest of the Daisy line, costing about a dollar and a half. It did not have a leather thong like Red's gun or his signature carved into the stock. But I loved it just the same. It worked faithfully for years and years. In fact, it never broke down. I would take it out after months of not using it and it would ping out those B-Bs unfailingly.

My father was something of a gun enthusiast and I don't think I had to talk him into getting me an air rifle very hard. As I recall, he had to convince my mother that it would be a good thing for me to have one. He was a tough old bird, sixty-eight when I was born, lean, mustached, with a jaw as square as Dick Tracy's and eyes that would cow many would-be tough guys. He carried a gun most of the time, usually a Colt Peacemaker (but a .38, not the famous .45).

Although his own cut of the pie could not have been very large, he would sometimes carry several thousand dollars in cash on him to cover expenses for his construction company. More than once, he had to use that gun to defend the money from hold-up men. My father was not the type of man to withhold an air rifle from his son.

In his book, *In God We Trust—All Others Pay Cash,* Jean Shepherd tells how his mother kept warning him that he would put his eye out with a B-B gun if he ever got one. He promised faithfully he would not. His mother persisted that he would. But time wore on and nerves wore out and he finally got the gun. He took his first shot. Ping! The B-B ricocheted off a tin can and smashed one lens of his glasses, almost—but not quite—putting his eye out. The gun went on the shelf for a few years.

I never came close to breaking my glasses with a B-B, mainly because I never wore a pair. A few times I did get hit by a ricocheting ball, but all in all I survived with very few bruises.

Target practice quickly lost its appeal for me. There wasn't a whole lot you could do with the air rifle once you had it. Rumors flitted around that you could kill rabbits with an air rifle if you hit one just right, but it was difficult enough to bag them with a .22 rifle. Mainly, there was just the pride in possessing a rifle all your own.

My air rifle was faithfully polished and oiled. I added "tattoos" (actually decals) to it to make it look like a "real" Red Ryder carbine but, like Jean Shepherd's, it mainly stayed on the shelf.

A few years ago, my mother called me in Hollywood from our home town in Illinois to report that the house there had been burglarized. Some of the things that were stolen were that Colt Peacemaker my father used to carry and my old air rifle. I'm sure Red Ryder would say, "Things not earned by honest work ain't going to bring any satisfaction."

Vintage Daisy air rifles sell for $25 to as high as $200 for a Red Ryder carbine like new and in the original carton.

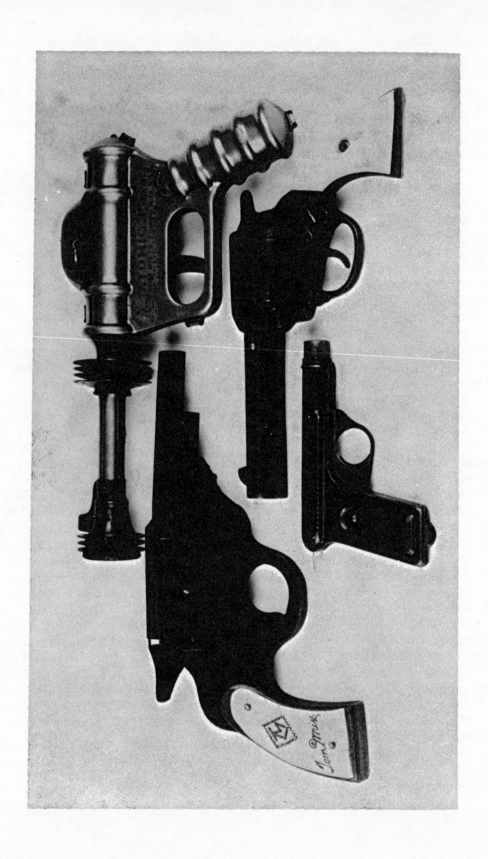

THINGS THAT GO BANG
IN THE AFTERNOON

When I was a very tiny tyke, cap guns were
very tiny silver-colored pistols that looked
nothing like a real gun. Some earlier models
(before *my* time, even) were cheap little tin
things, resembling sardine cans someone had
stepped on. After these first bite-size cast-iron
models, some of the first of the more realistic
cap pistols appeared.

Gene Autry's brand was on one of the first
of the life-size caliber. It was black iron with
white plastic "pearl" handles and had Gene's
signature in genuine simulated gold. Of course
it lacked the fine detail necessary to fool
anybody into thinking it was real, except perhaps
in a very dark alley. The drum of the Autry gun—
the round thing that holds the cartridges, as we
gun experts put it—did not revolve when you
cocked the gun or pulled the trigger. The drum
was just cast as a part of the one-piece metal.
The front was not even finished to look as if
blunt lead-nosed cartridges were lying in wait.
Inside the drum of the revolver that did not
revolve was hidden a roll of red paper caps on
a spoke. The line of paper was fed up through a
slot under the hammer and a lever pushed a new
cap into position each time you pulled the
trigger. This way you could fire your cap gun

almost as many times as Johnny Mack Brown or Rocky Lane fired their real ones in the Saturday matinees. Except, of course, that your gun would jam and have to be freed of acrid, blackened bits of paper.

Sometimes, however, the line of shredded paper would extend several inches above where your hammer fell on the caps. . . until one cap a bit more loaded than the rest would blow the ribbon of paper right in two. Or else you tore it off to preserve a more authentic appearance. After the battle was over you could explode even a supposedly dead cap by laying it on the concrete and socking it with a rock. (The sound of the exploding cap was never quite satisfactory. It usually was not loud enough. It made a sound like *SPUT!* Of course if the gun hammer hit it just right it went *KRACK!* But we could never get that "real" sound of the movies—*KERSH!* In the middle of a series of cap gun reports—*SPUT-SPUT-SPUT-KRACK-SPUT-CLICK* (that one didn't go off) *SPUT-SPUT*—we felt compelled to supply, through clenched teeth, our own *KERSH-KERSH!* (By the same token, we also felt it natural to supply our own hummed *adagio* to accompany the galloping of our imaginary horses.)

Cap guns reflected the times, the way other objects did. And so, by the fifties, toy sidearms were literally larger than lifesize, silvery and bejeweled with paste rubies and doughy diamonds. They looked absolutely nothing like anything one would use to shoot somebody. While I was a teenager, more interested in the latest issues of *Gala* and *Frolic,* I kept a dilettante's eye on the cap gun market. Most of those gaudy weapons carried the names of TV stars like Ward Bond of *Wagon Train* and Dale Robertson of *Tales of Wells Fargo.* Personally, I think the only TV star who would ever have actually carried a gun like that would have been Liberace.

The cap guns of today are no longer flashy. Quiet and efficient, they are almost exact copies of the real thing. It would not be hard to pull a liquor store holdup or a skyjacking with some of these guns. They have cylinders that turn when the trigger is pulled and appear loaded with lead-nosed cartridges. If that is not realistic enough, you can get CO_2 guns that fire pretty potent pellets and look real enough for Doc Holliday. It might even be a good idea to license them.

When I was a kid, if I did not have a cap gun I'd make a gun out of two clothespins. If I had no clothespins, there was always my trusty thumb and index finger and *KERSH-KERSH!* But unless your folks were *really* hit hard by the Depression, there were usually plenty of guns around.

Guns, guns, guns. There was an arsenal for every child to choose from. There were water pistols, in countless different shapes and sizes from scores of manufacturers. The *Little Orphan Annie* radio show offered one without any special markings which is nonetheless a sought-after collector's item today. The most valuable one is the Buck Rogers Disintegrator Pistol (which did not really disintegrate its victims but only inundated them with water). This can cost up to forty-five dollars today.

The guy up there in the 25th century also licensed a lot of other pistols, enough to start a whole Buck Rogers pistol range. All of them were variations on his ray gun—Rocket Pistols, Zap Guns and, after 1945, the Buck Rogers No. U-235 Atomic Pistol ("Absolutely HARMLESS," the Daisy Manufacturing Co. assured mothers).

Suction dart guns were another big item. You pulled the trigger and out shot a rubber-tipped dart that stuck fast to the bull's-eye target on the wall—or occasionally to the ceiling, where it would sometimes stubbornly hang for days, leaving its telltale mark that you had been shooting—against all the rules—in the house.

There were guns that punched holes in plain paper in a way that made it sound as if you had fired a cap (very popular during the World War Two restrictions on cap gun ammo). Other guns only shot rays of light—actually, they were just fancy flashlights. Lately guns have come on the market which shoot balls of compressed air to knock off hats and tip lampshades. One rifle produces its own sound of a ricochet.

All kids, or at least all boys, act out weapons fantasies. It is part of our animal heritage like fingernails and hair. In my time, it was not possible to resist group pressure towards playing with guns and still survive socially. In fact, I never knew a boy my age who refused to play with guns on religious or philosophical grounds, even those imposed on him by his parents. I don't think it's a good idea to try to suppress these gun fantasies when you are a kid. I suspect that those kids forced to read the Bible instead of playing with guns may have turned out even worse than the rest of us. Besides being an instrument for working off your aggressions, a kid's gun was a status symbol. If you had a big, half-dollar Gene Autry cap pistol, you walked taller than if you only had a little dinky nickel-plated thing labeled "Texas Buckeroo." Maybe it was teaching you materialistic acquisitiveness, but it also taught you that most people are acquisitive and that this is what you have to expect of the world.

The vainness and greed represent the bad side of it, but toy guns can also teach a kid about personal pride and style. When you were a kid and got a new gun and holster set (it smelled new—newly tanned leather and oil on iron) you did not think first of how you could play like you were killing someone (and children back then had a very hazy idea of death). No, you wondered how you would *look* in your gun belt. You wanted to carry the gun, and yourself, with style. The style carried over to the use of the gun—not shooting someone in the back, even in play, for instance.

Today, the youthfully cynical seem to try to deny that people act from any standards of morality. Nowhere is it more evident than in today's Western movies, where the "heroes" and "villains" are both so despicable that no thinking person could possibly have any emotional commitment to finding out what happened to the sons of bitches. But in real life, a king does give up his throne for the woman he loves. Every day cops turn down bribes, people pay honest debts, and writers refuse to write what they do not believe in. A small part of such things can be traced back to carrying a toy gun in the right style—not shooting people in the back and, most importantly, not fumbling and dropping it on your toe.

Yet I must say that, so far, I have never tried to rationalize my childish fascination with things that poked and punctured by going on to collect *real* guns. Carrying the things of childhood into your adult life can be taken *too* far.

BE A SUPERMAN!

CARRY THIS OFFICIAL SUPERMAN KRYPTO-RAYGUN

CLARK KENT (SUPERMAN) shoots actual pictures of the robbery—on the courtroom wall—with his KRYPTO-RAYGUN. This visual evidence CONVICTS the crook!

OFFICIAL SUPERMAN FILMS

No. 195: Reforming The Prison—Foiling Football Crooks—Killing The Cab Racket.

No. 209: The Subway Mystery—Saving The Circus—One Man Police Force. Each 28-scene FILM tells complete SUPERMAN story. Order Sets by numbers listed.

25c Per Set of 3 Films

GET ONE FOR XMAS!

Yes, be a Superman! Carry Daisy's new, harmless OFFICIAL SUPERMAN KRYPTO-RAYGUN . . . an exact replica of the RAYGUN Superman always carries concealed on his person in his fight against crime! Looks exactly like the KRYPTO-RAYGUN Superman had made of KRYPTONITE, the amazing metal from his birthplace—the weird Planet KRYPTON! Superman has no difficulty gathering pictures of his actual crook-chasing adventures. Then (disguised as CLARK KENT, reporter) he appears in court before the judge and jury and projects scenes from the crime on the courtroom wall with Superman's KRYPTO-RAYGUN. This picture evidence proves the guilt of the crooks.

SAFE! HARMLESS! FUN!

Daisy has created a genuine electric pocket projector (complete with lens, bulb, battery, and Superman Adventure Film) which does not "take pictures", but PROJECTS PICTURES! This OFFICIAL Superman KRYPTO-RAYGUN—now ready for you—actually projects one scene from an exciting 28-frame Superman Adventure Story each time you pull the trigger. Shoots each picture on the wall or ceiling or any smooth, light surface. Positively safe—absolutely harmless. A thrilling fun! An exact duplicate of Superman's real KRYPTO-RAYGUN in style, appearance, and size. Superman's name and picture is "engraved" on every OFFICIAL model. Get YOUR Daisy OFFICIAL SUPERMAN KRYPTO-RAYGUN at your nearest Department Store in 50c or $1 Outfits. If Dealer hasn't them, or no Dealer near you, order direct from Daisy, enclosing price, bills or Money Order—and we'll rush your order postpaid. Order all merchandise BY NUMBERS ONLY, as listed on this page.

No. 94: Beautiful SUPER-PACKAGE contains OFFICIAL Superman Krypto-Raygun, bulb, battery, real lenses, 7 complete Superman Film Stories of 28 different scenes each—a total of 196 pictures! Projects a new scene each time you pull trigger! Complete Outfit only _____ **$1**

No. 95: Carton holds OFFICIAL Superman Krypto-Raygun, bulb, battery, real lenses, one 28-frame Superman Film Adventure Story. Complete Outfit only _____ **50c**

$1.00

AT YOUR DEALERS
or write for Free Catalog

DAISY TOYS featuring the GENUINE OFFICIAL Equipment SUPERMAN the MIGHTY MAN OF TOMORROW

JUST OUT! PISTOL-DARTS

NEW Fun Game! Number 51

Put a cork dart into Pistol, pull trigger and, with a loud POP, dart flies and sticks to Target! New Daisy game comes with 2 long-barreled Target Pistols, 6 Harmless Gelatin-Tipped Darts, Target, Boxed—only 50¢

HARMLESS! 50¢

NEW DAISY PROJECTOR PISTOLS

No. 90 (Illustrated): Outfit contains 7 assorted wild west, comics, adventure, educational film stories (196 pictures), Projector Pistol, bulb., battery, real lenses—all for only _____ **$1**

No. 91: Same Complete Daisy Projector-Pistol equipment as in No. 90 but with only ONE 28-frame film. Complete _____ **50c**

NEW DAISY PEEP-SHOW PISTOLS

No. 96 (Illustrated): Peek thru rear pistol lens—SEE show inside pistol day or night. A real "pocket theatre", Pistol, 28-view SUPERMAN Film, all in carton. Only _____ **25c**

No. 92: Same pistol as No. 96 but with selected 28-view film instead of SUPERMAN film, in carton _____ **25c**

Assorted Film Subjects **25c PER SET AS LISTED**

Films fit every RAYGUN, Projector Pistol and Peep-Show Pistol advertised here. Sold only in Sets of 1, 2, or 3 films. Each film has 28 frames. NO variation from sets as listed.

No. 25: Robinson Crusoe—Peter Rabbit—Pilot Ferry Makes Good. **No. 45:** Wild Animals—Night Before Xmas—Little Black Sambo. **No. 55:** Tom Dulcode—Treasure Island—Day on a Ranch. **No. 65:** Rocius Rides a Mule—Ships of the World—A Day at the Circus. **No. 75:** Justice Rides the Range—President of the U. S.—Hansel & Gretel. **No. 85:** Dogs—3 Little Pigs—Victory Seas. **No. 95:** Little Red Hen—Little Red Riding Hood—Gingerbread Boy. **No. 105:** The Pilgrims—Cortez in Mexico—Development of Locomotive in America. **No. 125:** Bunky Goes Hunting—Rich in the Jungle—Miggy, Mutch & Toby Toothpick. **No. 115:** Dan Dryce Forks, Yellowstone and Grand Canyon Parks. **No. 145:** Tom Sawyer—Daniel Boone and the Indians—Rip Van Winkle and the Dwarfs. **No. 165:** Spooks—The Dance of Mr. Bones—The Haunted House. **No. 175:** Farm Animals—Strange Birds—The Eagle's Nest. **No. 185** (2 films): Seeing New York, Series A and B. **No. 215:** The Three Bears—Tom Dulwell. Episode No. 2. COLORED FILMS (1 film to a set). **No. 520:** National Parks of West. **No. 530:** Hansel & Gretel. **No. 540:** Tom Sawyer.

Duty added in Canada to all prices on this page.

Made By The Manufacturers of Famous Daisy Air Rifles

DAISY MANUFACTURING COMPANY 6812 Union St., PLYMOUTH, MICHIGAN, U. S. A.

149

WHERE TO BUY IT

All the fabled items described in this book—Captain Midnight badges, Tom Mix rings, Superman comic books, Shadow magazines—are for sale by professional dealers. Every item is not in stock at all times, but if you follow a few dealers' lists for some months, you are sure to find the *area* of your interest (such as Jack Armstrong premiums). If, on the other hand, your want item is very specific—a Tom Mix "look-in" Mystery Ring or *Captain Marvel Adventures* No. 5—finding it may perhaps require years of looking.

Prices of the items vary from dealer to dealer, from time to time. These days they do not vary fantastically—the price range of a hypothetical item might be from $17 to $25, not from fifty cents to fifty dollars. In general, prices are steadily going up, with no reason to believe they will drop. Condition varies from dealer to dealer too. Such terms as "mint" and "very good" are merely opinions stated by the dealer. Dealers often are human enough to err in their favor by overestimating an item from "fair" to "good," from "good" to "very good." Actually, grading has tended to become overly charitable, so that a "fair" item would look pretty poor to the average person.

No dealers listed here are known to take a customer's money without forwarding merchandise. They may not have been able to satisfy everyone 100% of the time on delivery speed, condition, etc., but in my opinion they are reliable.

Some dealers in the nostalgia field handle a little bit of everything—although perhaps primarily old comic books because the most money can be made there. Besides comics, they deal in radio premiums, movie posters, old pulp magazines, old toys, etc. Their inventories constantly change, of course.

MULTIPLE DEALERS

David Alexander, P.O. Box 2921, Hollywood, Calif. 90028.

Bond Street Book Store, Steve Edrington and Jim McDonald, proprietors, 1638 N. Wilcox Ave., Hollywood, Calif. 90028.

Cherokee Book Shop, Inc., Jack Blum, proprietor; Burt Blum, Comics Department; Gene Blum, Hardcover Dept.; Oliver Dernberger, Movie Department; 6607 Hollywood Blvd., Hollywood, Calif. 90028.

Collector's Book Store, Malcolm Willets and Len Brown, proprietors, 6763 Hollywood Blvd., Hollywood, Calif. 90028.

Claude Held, P.O. Box 140, Buffalo, N.Y. 14225.

Howard Rogofsky, P.O. Box 1102, Linden Hill Sta., Flushing, N.Y. 11354.

Phil Seuling, 621 Avenue Z, Brooklyn, N.Y. 11223.

Bill Thailing, P.O. Box 352, Willow Station, Cleveland, Ohio.

These are among the dealers with the largest catalogs, doing the most business. There are, of course, thousands of other smaller dealers.

RADIO TAPE DEALERS

Most of the old radio shows mentioned in this book—*Tom Mix, Jack Armstrong, I Love a Mystery, Edgar Bergen and Charlie McCarthy*—as well as virtually every other favorite old show is available from hundreds of dealers. Most of these radio tape dealers are offering copies of shows they obtained from other collectors—some actually copies of copies of copies, dozens of generations away from the source—a transcription disc recording, in most cases. The following dealers are known to offer shows which they "originated" from the old discs, thus offering clear, good fidelity recordings (although some shows now exist only in "Very Good" or "Good" condition). The standard recording method is four-track reel-to-reel, although two-track, cassettes, etc. are available at other rates.

Radio Yesteryear, David Goldin, proprietor, Box H, Croton-on-Hudson, N.Y. Rates: $12 per recorded hour.

Remember Radio, Inc., Don Maris, proprietor, Box 2513, Norman, Okla. 73069. Rates: 6 hours for $8. (The six hours is in one set of several shows—usually 12 half-hour programs—unlike Radio Yesteryear, which allows you to pick any shows in their catalog for its higher hourly rate.)

Jim Harmon, P.O. Box 38612, Hollywood, Calif. 90038. Rates: 6 hours for $9, or 4 hours for $7.50. (These rates include pre-selected sets, but may be made up of two- and three-hour units. Harmon delivers more slowly than some others, since—like hundreds of others—he is only a part-time radio tape dealer.)

RADIO PREMIUM & OLD TOY DEALERS

Ted Hake, 115 S. 21st St., Philadelphia, Pa. 19103.

Jack Melcher, 2105 Indian Rd., Waukegan, Ill. 60085. (Mr. Melcher also publishes a fanzine, *Radio Premium Collectors' Newsletter,* bimonthly, $3 per year.)

Nickelodeon (a store), Ed and Elaine Levin, 13826 Ventura Blvd., Sherman Oaks, Calif. 91403.

MOVIE POSTERS & MOVIE MEMORABILIA

Larry Edmunds Book Shop, 6658 Hollywood Blvd., Hollywood, Calif. 90028.

RARE BOOKS

Roy A. Squires, 1745 Kenneth Rd., Glendale, Calif. 91201. (Besides searching out rare issues of *Weird Tales* and hardcover books of such fantasy authors as Robert E. Howard, Mr. Squires also publishes exquisite examples of the bookmaker's art—pamphlets of Howard, Lovecraft, Bradbury, and others in editions of perhaps 300 copies for $5 each.)

MISCELLANEOUS

Finders-Seekers, Manny Weltman, proprietor, 13639 Sylvan St., Van Nuys, Calif. 91401. (Mr. Weltman will search out—for a fee— any radio premium, comic book, or what-have-you.)